T0243274

AFTER THE TAMPA

AFTER THE TAMPA

From Afghanistan to New Zealand

ABBAS NAZARI

ALLEN&UNWIN
SYDNEY·MELBOURNE·AUCKLAND·LONDON

First published in 2021

Copyright © Abbas Nazari, 2021
Images © author's private collection unless otherwise credited on page.

Allen & Unwin
Level 2, 10 College Hill
Auckland 1011, New Zealand
Phone: (64 9) 377 3800

Email: info@allenandunwin.com
Web: www.allenandunwin.co.nz

83 Alexander Street
Crows Nest NSW 2065, Australia
Phone: (61 2) 8425 0100

A catalogue record for this book is available
from the National Library of New Zealand

ISBN 978 1 988547 64 0

Design by Megan van Staden
Cover photo by Juan Zarama Perini
Set in 13/19 pt Goudy Old Style
Printed and bound by McPhersons Printing Co. Ltd

10 9 8 7 6 5

MIX
Paper from
responsible sources
FSC® C001695
www.fsc.org

The paper in this book is FSC® certified.
FSC® promotes environmentally responsible,
socially beneficial and economically viable
management of the world's forests.

To Mum and Dad
Thank you for giving up your today for our tomorrow.

OUT BEYOND IDEAS OF
WRONGDOING AND RIGHTDOING,
THERE IS A FIELD. I'LL MEET YOU THERE.
— RUMI

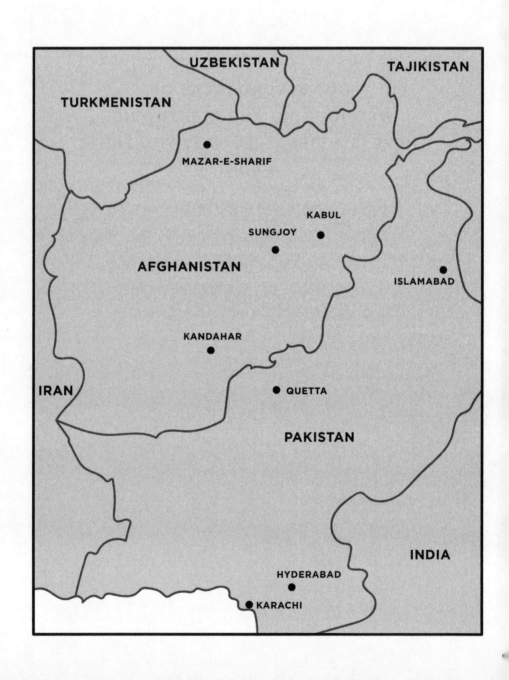

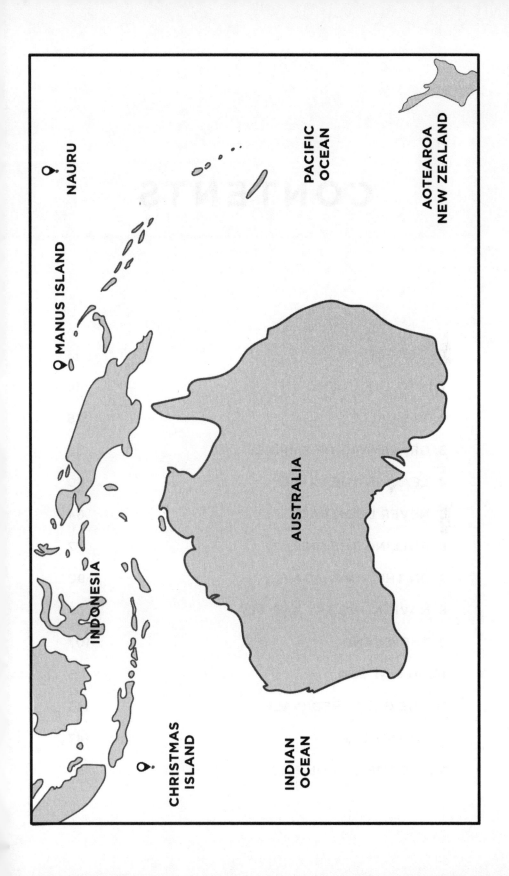

NAURU

MANUS ISLAND

PACIFIC OCEAN

AOTEAROA
NEW ZEALAND

INDONESIA

AUSTRALIA

CHRISTMAS
ISLAND

INDIAN
OCEAN

CONTENTS

CONTENTS

PROLOGUE

I WILL BE the first to admit I have not personally accomplished anything worthy of writing a book about. I have not built a billion-dollar company, or won an Olympic gold medal, or summitted some great mountain. In fact the most interesting thing I've done is receive a scholarship to an American university. So when I was asked to write a book about my life I felt like a fraud.

What story would I tell?

Would anyone be remotely interested in what I had to say?

But as I thought about it more, I realised there was a story I could tell. A story that deserves to be chronicled. So this book is not about the life and times of Abbas Nazari.

It has my name on the cover, but the story belongs to all of the 433 asylum seekers who were rescued from drowning in the Indian Ocean by the Norwegian container ship, the *Tampa*.

Twenty years on from those harrowing events this story is more relevant than ever. As the world's refugee crisis deepens, no one can ignore the plight of the thousands of desperate people fleeing their various war-torn homelands.

At events where I am asked to speak, I am astounded by the feedback I receive when I talk about this. Everyone has heard about refugees, but hardly anyone has ever met or got to know one personally. It's time they did.

I am Abbas Nazari. My family and I arrived in New Zealand as refugees rescued by the *Tampa*. I am proud to call myself a New Zealander.

Afghans are notoriously bad at writing things down, so I hope this book serves as a memoir of all the people who fled with us. Much of the detail comes from my childhood memory. For details of events during which I was not present or cannot recall clearly, I have relied on the memories of others present, such as my parents and other Tampa rescuees who were eventually resettled in New Zealand.

I am fortunate to be in a position where I can write a book about my journey. For the majority of refugees it is a very different story. This book is theirs too. It begins in Afghanistan but it could just as easily be Somalia, Syria, Nicaragua, Myanmar or any of the other conflict zones around the world.

It is the story of every refugee who has been desperate enough to pack up everything, leave home and friends, and set off into an unknown future. I hope that as you read it you are prompted to think about their plight.

The topic of refugees and asylum seekers provokes heated debate and passionate responses from people, but few who are party to such discussions have actually lived the refugee experience. Few know what it is like to uproot yourselves from your homeland, risk everything, then, if you are exceptionally lucky, be resettled in an utterly foreign land, learning to navigate a new hyphenated identity. What is that experience like? Do they ever hanker to return home?

I hope this book helps in some small way to shed light on a global issue facing humanity.

1.

INTO THE
UNKNOWN

'**WAKE UP! ABBAS,** wake up — we have to go now!' hissed Mum as she shook me. 'Get your things — the bus is here. Hurry!'

It was the middle of the night. I wiped my eyes and sprang to my feet. All around me my siblings and the other children were a swirling hurricane of activity in the dormitory. I reached for the one thing I could call mine, the small navy backpack Dad had bought me for school in Quetta. I folded the donated T-shirt and pants Mum had placed on my pillow and stuffed them inside. I was seven years old, and a few months after leaving Afghanistan my worldly possessions amounted to a backpack and two items of clothing. Fearing this would never be enough for whatever lay ahead I filled the empty space with anything I could lay my hands on. Some rubber bands. A fork. Two bananas. A pen. A plastic bag. A pair of socks.

As I did up my Velcro sandals I peered out the window into the dark and could make out a small bus parked to the side of the main gate to the dormitories. A grizzled man with his belly hanging out of his shirt stood by the bus door, counting people as they boarded. A wiry figure was helping load the bags. They were sweating, with dark circles under their eyes as if they hadn't slept for weeks. They didn't look at all friendly.

'Hurry or there won't be any seats left for us,' said Mum, urging me down the stairs.

Dad helped load luggage into the undercarriage while Mum whispered a prayer. My baby brother Mojtaba was wrapped tightly in a blanket under her arm, while her other hand held my sister Shekufah's. Big brothers Ali and Sakhi were looking around hopefully for their friends. Surrounded by my family, I was not frightened, just excited that we were finally getting out of this horrible place.

The curtains on the bus were all closed. Once everybody was on board the engine roared to life, the headlights turned on and we were on our way. I fell asleep almost immediately as the bus glided silently through the city streets.

Some hours later I was jolted awake for the second

time that night. The city lights had been replaced by a thick jungle of coconut palms on either side. The smooth asphalt had given way to a bumpy dirt road. As the bus rattled along a few people started vomiting. A sign of things to come.

'Quiet!' hissed the wiry man. 'Nearly there.' He put his fingers to his lips.

We drove a little further down the dirt road until we reached a clearing. The unmistakable sound of crashing waves told us we were at the coast, but the night was so dark I couldn't see where land ended and the sea began.

The bus stopped and the wiry man got up, clutching a fat yellow envelope. He put his finger to his lips again, gesturing to us to remain quiet, then disappeared into the jungle. After a few moments he returned, minus the envelope. The driver restarted the engine and began to move again.

Silence hung in the humid tropical night. As we drove on, the jungle thinned, then receded completely on one side, revealing a black canvas. The ocean. We were in a clearing near the edge of a cliff about 30 metres above the sea. The bus drew closer to the cliff edge, so its headlights illuminated the waters below. A wooden fishing boat, perhaps twice as big as our bus, was tied to a rock with thick ropes. It rose on every wave, scraping the rocks and tautening the ropes with every push and pull.

Surely this was not our ship. There must have been a mistake.

People began murmuring, looking incredulous. We had been promised a luxurious all-metal vessel where every family would have their own cabin. Whoever's boat this was, it was not ours. Ours must be on its way. We got off the bus and Dad helped out with the suitcases again.

As we gathered our bags, two full-sized buses pulled up. I watched as dozens of people began streaming out. How many would there be? They could not all be in our party. Perhaps there was more than one boat? Maybe this boat was for them, and ours was still coming? Yes, that would be it.

As each bus emptied, the driver would do a U-turn and drive away to allow another minivan or bus to pull up. There were hundreds of people. The nervous chatter grew as more arrived.

The wiry man and our driver pointed to the boat before turning our bus around and disappearing. Dad looked around and recognised a few of the men from other buses.

'It looks like that might be for us,' said one of the men; it was more of a question than a statement.

'Let's go down and see if there are other boats coming,' said another.

I held on to Mum's hand as we walked in the darkness down the steep, rocky hillside towards the boat, sea spray in our faces.

We stood on a patch of sand by the water's edge, a few metres from the boat. Up close, it was exactly as it had appeared from above. An old wooden fishing boat, its paint flaking away to reveal wooden beams and rotting timber. Barnacles clung to its belly.

About half a dozen men emerged on deck, waving for us to climb aboard. A flimsy wooden ladder hung down one side, its legs submerged in the sea, while a rope net was fastened next to it.

This was our boat. There was no doubt about it.

Excitement gave way to fear — and then anger.

'This is not what I paid for!' shouted one man at the crew on deck, breaking the silence. 'This is not what I was promised.'

Whispered murmurs became angry shouts as more people echoed his disbelief. Women began wailing as they realised the truth; children began crying.

A few families who had gathered near the ship backed away, the adults arguing energetically among themselves.

'There is no way on God's earth I will get on that boat. I will not allow my children near that thing.'

'There are holes in its sides! And look how many

people there are. This boat cannot hold all of us!'

'We've made it this far. Let's just wait for the next boat –
a better one. I don't mind waiting weeks or even months – I
just cannot get on that thing.'

The conversations continued for what seemed like
hours. Eventually a few families, led by the women, began
wandering back to the clearing. Meanwhile, a group of
men gathered near the boat, whispering. I followed Dad as
he joined the circle.

'Brothers, we have a choice to make. Either we get on
or we go home – it's that simple,' said one man.

'Get on? How do you expect me to take my family onto
that thing!' replied another.

'What's the alternative? You have emptied your pockets
buying the tickets. If you stay you will end up homeless on
the streets, begging for food. Is that what you want for
your family?'

'I want my family alive!'

A few of the men seemed resigned and had climbed
aboard.

'The boat looks old on the outside but it's in good
shape inside. Perhaps it has enough bones to carry us to
Australian waters.'

Soon enough a sizeable portion of the group had
convinced themselves the boat was seaworthy. If they

weren't convinced, they pretended otherwise.

Alhamdulillah. Thank God.

I looked at the water as the conversation in our group raged on. I had seen the ocean from the plane when we flew in to Jakarta, but this was the closest I had ever been. It was a thick, honey-like syrup, black as midnight.

'Dad, what do we do?'

'I don't know, son. Only God knows.'

We walked back to our family group.

'Abdul, we can't do this!' said Mum. It was one of the few times I had heard her call Dad by his first name. She was serious.

'You knew it would always come down to this. That we would make it all this way and then we would have to decide what to do. Well, we're here now.'

'I *can't*,' she pleaded. 'Look at your family. How could you live with yourself if one of us died?'

'And how could I live with myself if all of us died begging on the streets here in Indonesia?'

The thought of living in a refugee camp so far away from home struck Mum silent.

'Have faith,' said her husband. 'We have made it this far.'

WHEN WE SEE a trail of desperate people fleeing conflict, perhaps on the television news, we miss the points in time when a parent has to make a life-altering decision on behalf of a whole family. To stay or to go? To endure known misery or to march towards an unknown future?

Caught between the endless ocean and an uncertain earth, we chose life. Some kind of future beckoned and desperation powered us to climb aboard.

It seemed everyone was coming to the same conclusion and a mild scramble erupted. Luggage was tossed on board in a swarm of activity. Noise. Chaos. Crying children. Adults waded out nervously, most touching seawater for the first time in their lives.

Today my mother recalls the curtain of fear that hung before her as she walked towards the boat. She battled with the voice in her head that insistently urged her to stay on dry land. To cling to certainty, however bleak. With every step she felt she was dragging a heavy chain. Through teary eyes she could hardly see the ladder as her feet, one by one, left solid ground.

Dad remained calm. Stoic, even. If he was fearful, he did not show it. He knew he had played his hand and the rest was outside his control. It was all in God's hands now.

The ocean laid out a welcome mat, black as obsidian.

We followed the other families, climbing down a hatch

on the deck to the enclosed level below. Dad claimed a spot to one side in the bow, near one of the wooden pillars supporting the upper deck. Other families piled in around us until every centimetre of timber was occupied. There wasn't much vertical clearance, and Dad had to hunch over to avoid cracking his head on the rafters. I sat with my knees folded into my chest, my back against Ali's. We were packed like a box of dates. It was pitch black inside, save for some light streaming in from the lone hatch. It felt as if we had been swallowed by a great beast.

To this day I have no idea whether everyone waiting boarded or if some turned back in the end. But when it seemed that everyone who had decided to come was on board, the commotion died down. The sound of a diesel engine started up, loud enough to drown the crash of the waves. We were moving.

A few hours earlier I had been asleep on the floor of a dormitory room with my family. Now we were in an even smaller space with what seemed like half the population of Jakarta. As we motored away from the reef, the first rays of daylight illuminated the previously seamless joint where sky met sea. Behind us the dark shape of the island grew into a vivid green before fading out of sight. The ocean was now a deep blue.

There was no turning back now.

2.
THE
VALLEY

'**DON'T LET IT** get away!' yelled my big brother Ali.

'I'm trying, but it's too fast!' I replied between rapid breaths.

'I'll beat you up if you lose it!'

'Why are we even collecting more? Your jar is full anyway!'

'Because I want to show that I'm the best collector in the village. Now get it!'

My hands gently wrapped around the *khirsug* like an eggshell protecting life within. I carried it over to Ali, who slowly unscrewed the lid of his jar.

'That makes eighteen! I am the king!' shouted Ali, carefully rewrapping the container of glowing beetles in a soft cloth that he tied around his waist like a belt.

'Come on, let's go and show the others. They'll be so jealous!'

Ali and I walked through the woods and down the valley to the village. It was dusk, that golden hour when everything is coated in a honey-like glaze. Our house came in to view, perched high on the hillside across the valley.

It was typical of houses in the area. Rectangular clay walls reinforced with wheat husks, and wooden beams that protruded at either end of the flat roof. I could see the door between the rows of apricot and cherry trees. As we came nearer I could hear the gentle mooing of the cows as they settled in for the night, under an awning that jutted out from one side of the house. With winter coming, Dad would soon close off the awning with a tarpaulin. The bitter cold and heavy snow would otherwise be too much for the two cows, the donkey and chickens who called it home.

On the hill beyond our house I could see the glimmering golden dome of the local *masjid* (mosque) catching the last rays of the day. Below our house lay the rest of the village, a patchwork quilt of rectangular clay houses with flat roofs stepped down the side of the hill to the lush valley floor.

The houses seemed to converge on the alpine creek that twisted and turned its way through the valley. Fed by rain and snow from faraway mountains, this creek was the life source for our village. It allowed people to grow crops, make tea, nourish their animals, wash their clothes, and swim during the boiling-hot summers. Like a ribbon around a gift, it held the villagers in a common bond.

The distribution of water from the creek was highly regulated. Every family that owned a patch of land also enjoyed a water right, with the allocated amount depending on the position and size of their plot. A series of individual canals had been dug by hand from the creek to everyone's little plot of land. When it was time, a family would send someone with a shovel to dig into the canal wall, creating an opening to allow the water to their plot. Then they would close off the canal to the previous family's plot. It was vital that each family timed the change exactly, as missing a shift meant someone else's crops would be overwatered and yours would go thirsty. Because the water never stopped, it meant all families from time to time experienced the joy of staying up late or waking up early to change the flow. I recall many nights following Dad down to the valley floor, him holding a shovel in one hand and an oil lamp in the other.

Life in our village at 2000 metres above sea level was simple, idyllic — and now seems like a world away. Tucked away in the foothills of the Hindu Kush mountains in the

Afghan province of Ghazni, Sungjoy is a cluster of small villages in the district of Jaghuri. About a hundred families lived in Sungjoy.

The Afghan family is extensive and multigenerational, with siblings and their families generally living together under one roof. One family may consist of dozens of people. Afghanistan has never held a comprehensive census. The last attempt was in 1979 but it was never finished, so every government statistic is based on estimates and projections. The best estimates would show that there were about 3000 people in Sungjoy when we lived there.

Like most villages in the highlands of Afghanistan, and indeed many parts of the world, Sungjoy took its name from its most prominent geographical feature: the creek that flowed from the rocky mountains and through the valley. Sungjoy translates as Rock (*sung*) Creek (*joy*). The English translations of the names of most towns in the area would fit well on Tolkien's map of Middle-earth. There is Siyah-Sung (Black Rock), Sar-e Qol (River Head), Anguri (Grapeville), Koh-e Sefid (White Mountain) and my favourite: Koh-e Nalah (Echo Mountain).

Life in Sungjoy was a never-ending battle between humans and the elements.

In the spring, the hillside would transform from dark brown to patches of green growth that would delight the shepherds. We would hike up the mountains in search of *chukree*, a wild plant that tasted like a cross between celery and rhubarb. Finding a big bush meant an afternoon's worth of cutting, peeling and chewing the deliciously sour and juicy stalks. Armed with slingshots, we would pass the time by hunting lizards and snakes. We would wait for them to emerge from between rocks, tilting their bodies to soak up the sun, only to see death coming in the form of a pebble. Some superstitious folk would bury a lizard's tail for fear that it would otherwise resurrect itself as a snake if left in the sun.

We would escape the blazing summer sun and dust storms by staying inside or swimming in the creek. At some point, someone had piled enough rocks and dirt in the water to create a small swimming pool. We would tightly tie our trouser legs and drawstring waists so that the garment would act as a buoy, helping us stay afloat. With no electricity, the only way to get a decent night's sleep in the heat was to sleep on the roof, under a blanket of stars.

In autumn, the valley would light up with brilliant foliage, a flurry of fire red and rusty orange. We would spend the cool evenings chasing *khirsug* and play games to stave off boredom. Our games included marbles and, my personal favourite, *shighay baazi*, a game similar to dice but played with the knucklebone of a cow or sheep.

Games involving marksmanship were popular. Adults played *sung-geerug*, a throwing game that involves teams of men throwing a rock at a marker, like aerial lawn bowls. Children preferred the traditional slingshot. Our target was usually a tree or rock or an unlucky bird or lizard. Although I was a natural with the slingshot, I was hopeless with the *palkho*, a long sling that one would swing above the head and release at a precise moment, rocketing a stone out from the pouch. The shepherd boys were experts at *palkho* and could redirect their flock simply by aiming a stone at a particular point beside the animals.

Winter was my favourite season. In the highlands of Afghanistan, winter means heavy snow. We would wake up to see a blanket of snow covering every inch of the valley, as if God had spilt a giant bucket of white paint. Some mornings were so cold the banks of the creek would freeze, and there would be a winter wonderland of icicles hanging from branches and half-submerged logs. With no plumbing, women would trudge through the snow in a shawl and some fabric shoes to collect water. Mum said green tea tasted much better when you'd had to work for it.

On big snow days everyone had a job to do. Shovels and rakes in hand, we would climb to the roof and begin shovelling snow. Although the clay and straw mixture was generally water-resistant, if the snow was left to melt it would seep through and rot the timber beams. Once the roof was cleared, we would clear a footpath to the stables, neighbouring homes, and on to common areas, including to the well, the cemetery and the *masjid*. It was a communal effort, and we would shout across to neighbours to see if they needed a hand.

Most houses had a simple underground heating system whereby heat from the *tandoor* oven would be channelled underneath the floor to other parts of the house. A slab of rock in one corner of the living room was a makeshift heater. We would sit around the slab, drinking tea and wolfing down warm naan. It was not much, but it was enough.

In ours as in most Afghan households, everything was done together, and it was always all hands on deck. At mealtimes everyone sat cross-legged around a mat on the floor. After dinner we would all gather around Dad to hear folktales of the bumbling Mullah Nasreddin. Come nightfall, we would arrange mattresses, pillows and blankets on the floor of the living room to sleep, lined up like vehicles in a carpark. Children would walk to school together, while the adults spent every waking moment tending to their land and animals.

There's a Hazara saying — *naan qad piyaz, ba qash-e waaz*, which means 'bread and onion with open brows'. It is a simple saying that perfectly encapsulates our life in the highlands in the 1990s. We did not have much but were grateful for the little we did have. We simply got on with the task of living and making do. While Afghan cities enjoyed electricity, plumbing, television and other trappings of modernity, such progress had not made it to Sungjoy. The isolation provided by the mountains produced a hardy, resourceful and resilient people.

The villagers had seen their share of hardship over the years. My father spoke of a childhood spent in a constant search for food. Dad was a stoic, broad-shouldered man. He was born in 1955 when Zahir Shah, the last king of Afghanistan, was still in charge. My grandparents both died from tuberculosis when my father and his two brothers were teenagers, so they were forced to start working, taking any job that would put food on the table.

My father's teenage years were incredibly difficult, and this has shaped his outlook on life. From about 1969 to 1972 Afghanistan, in particular the central highlands of Hazarajat, was struck by a deep famine. Afghans of my parents' generation remember this period well. Food was so scarce that my father recalls many villagers boiling wild plants, catching mice or mixing sawdust with their wheat. The vicious cycle of poverty struck the communities of Hazarajat, already facing decades of underinvestment, most acutely. This left a generation of Afghans, including my father and his brothers, without formal education or pathways to employment. When my grandparents passed away, my father and uncles had to beg and borrow the few rupees to purchase a coffin for them. I can understand now why my father has always insisted that we finish our plates. Sources suggest that as many as 500,000 Afghans, a disproportionate amount of them Hazara, died of starvation or related causes during this period. The lack of response from the central government precipitated the major political unrest of the 1970s, which would pave the way for the decades of conflict to come.

While drought and famine wrecked Afghanistan, neighbouring Iran was booming. My father, like tens of thousands of other Afghans, crossed the border into Iran in search of work. They laboured on construction sites, working from sunrise to sunset in mostly miserable conditions. It wasn't just the physical demands of the work that got to them; it was also the non-stop racial abuse and harassment they experienced from Iranian foremen, many of whom were quick to express their disdain for the poor, uneducated immigrants from across the border. Dad and his workmates endured the blatant racism across every worksite they were at. Answering back would have been counter-productive; they kept their heads down and got on with the job.

After some months my father found work at a large timber-processing facility. Kar-Khaana-e-Chob, known as the Timber Factory, was an American-funded venture churning out timber for construction. Dad recalls walking in as a teenager and immediately feeling at home. What he lacked in formal education, he made up for with manual skill. He learnt the tools quickly and could soon wield a hammer better than most. One of the American supervisors later wrote Dad a letter of recommendation attesting to his abilities as a fine carpenter. Dad knew he was on to a good thing and went about bringing his brothers and other Jaghuri workers to the Timber Factory, far away from the abuse of the Iranians. They revelled in the work, finding joy in the dignity it gave them. The American foremen were fair and honest.

Around the Eid New Year's festival the men would journey back to Jaghuri. At the ripe old age of 21, my father married my mother, who was five years his junior. The newlyweds settled in the bottom level of the homestead in Sungjoy. But within two months of the wedding Dad, along with many of the other men of the village, left again for Iran. Driven by hunger and desperation, they had to make the most of the opportunity while the going was good. The first years of my parents' marriage were spent like this — between worlds. The men would come home once a year, bringing their savings in wads of cash stuffed in the lining of their jackets.

Within a few years my father and uncles had saved enough to ensure they never went hungry again, and they had a plan. They had become used to cars and trucks in Iran, but Sungjoy was still using donkeys for transport. The brothers became the first locals to buy a lorry, a rusty old Soviet Kamaz. With this they began travelling between the different districts of Ghazni, carrying people, food, medical supplies and other goods across the province.

Newly married, and with cash in his pocket, my father dreamed of having a family and maybe even moving to the city. The world was at his feet.

3.
GRAVEYARD
OF EMPIRES

LIKE A PATCHWORK quilt, Afghanistan is a multi-ethnic and multi-lingual country. The Afghan Constitution makes specific mention of fourteen distinct ethnic groups, and eight languages. No single ethnic group is big enough to form an outright majority, but each are unique in history, culture and geography. My people, the Hazara, make up about 10–20 per cent of the Afghan population.

The Hazara are ethnically Asian, with physical features typically found in Central Asia. Dari, a dialect of Farsi, is the native language, and the vast majority of Hazara follow the Islamic Shi'a faith, rather than the majority Sunni sect. A largely oral-based culture, origin stories are wide and lacking in critical scholarship. Some point to the Buddhas of Bamiyan as proof that people with Asian features have been present in what is now Afghanistan since the sixth century. Others contend that the Hazara are descendants of nomadic Turkic tribes from Persia and further west. Although there are no universally accepted theories of where the Hazara came from or how they came to be in Afghanistan, the most popular story is that the word Hazara is from the Farsi *hazaar*, meaning one thousand. The legend goes that Genghis Khan, in conquering Afghanistan in the thirteenth century, left one thousand soldiers and their families to seize and populate the area. Gradually those thousand Mongols interbred and mingled with various nomadic tribes to create the Hazara ethnic group. Over the centuries the Hazara settled in the highlands of the Hindu Kush mountains, an area that would later become part of central Afghanistan. They named this area Hazarajat — the land of the Hazara.

Geography is destiny, and in no place is this truer than in Afghanistan. Geography has rendered Afghanistan a mountainous land bridge connecting empires and civilisations spanning Central and South Asia, the Middle East and China. Consequently, Afghan history, culture, cuisine and ethno-cultural diversity has been influenced by the movement of people and ideas across this part of the world. As a result, Afghanistan has been a stage for constant warring between these disparate groupings. Through much of the nineteenth century Afghanistan also served as a buffer between Czarist Russia to the north and the British-controlled Indian subcontinent to the south. Over successive Anglo–Afghan wars in the nineteenth century Afghanistan's territories were consolidated as a new nation began to form.

Meanwhile, by the late nineteenth century Abdur Rahman Khan had begun to assert dominance across Afghanistan's domestic politics under the umbrella of Islam. It is important to note that while Islam had been dominant for centuries in the land that would become Afghanistan, other faiths had been widely practised too, including Buddhism, Judaism, Zoroastrianism, Sufism and several forms of mysticism. Faith practices varied between and within ethnic groups, and even between clan groups within tribes.

Khan instituted a policy of Sunni Pashtun nationalism, and set about broadening his reach from Kabul to the highlands. Known as the Iron Emir for his tendency to crush rebellions, he launched an all-out offensive on Hazarajat in 1892, starting a year-long campaign that would decimate the Hazara population. Although historical accounts vary, most sources suggest that more than half of Afghanistan's Hazara were either killed or forced to flee as refugees.

One story that is enshrined in Hazara lore is the story of the *Chil Dukhtaran*, the Forty Daughters. As the Iron Emir's forces enclosed the Hazara of Uruzgan province, a group of young village girls who had witnessed the deaths of their parents sought refuge atop a mountain. With enemy forces closing in, they realised that only death could provide an escape from rape and torture, and so the girls all jumped to their deaths.

Following the Iron Emir's campaign, as many as 10,000 Hazara men and women were sold in Kabul's slave markets, adding further revenue to that gained from the plunder of Hazarajat. From this time, the racist oppression of the Hazara was ingrained in the emerging Afghan national psyche and government institutions, where it would sit firmly for the next century.

In fact the cruelty of the Iron Emir marked the beginning of a genocidal campaign that is still under way today. A place of relative safety and prosperity for centuries, Hazarajat became a seat of pain and anguish. Government funds were directed away, lands were confiscated, and the residents of Hazarajat saw their livelihoods collapse.

Following the third Anglo-Afghan war, Great Britain agreed that British India would not extend past the Khyber Pass and recognised Afghanistan's independence. The Anglo-Afghan Treaty of 1919 solidified Afghanistan's international borders and the newly independent country emerged into the community of nations. In the interwar period of the 1920s–30s, the advent of the motorcar opened Afghanistan to the world and to itself. Cities became connected by roads, and an age of mobility and education began to transform most of the country from a collection of tribes into a modern nation. But as the cities saw investment and development, Hazarajat was left behind, the benefits of modernisation circumventing the highlands.

The post–World War II period opened Afghanistan further to the world. Kabul became a fixture on the hippie route from London to Delhi. For foreigners streaming along the Silk Road it was an exotic blend of old and new, as if parallel universes had collided on the streets of Kabul. Markets selling ancient remedies, recipes and trinkets sat alongside chic stores advertising high-street fashion. If your grandparents travelled on the old Silk Road, they probably have an Afghan rug or two that they collected from the bazaars of Kabul and Mazar-e-Sharif.

Then Afghanistan, like many countries, found itself collateral damage in the Cold War. The Soviet-backed People's Democratic Party of Afghanistan (PDPA) mounted a coup d'état in 1978, and on Christmas Eve 1979 the first Soviet tanks rolled into Kabul. This marked the beginning of a fruitless decade-long effort by the Soviets to add Afghan to its growing list of -stans, and it provided another opportunity for Afghanistan to live up to its moniker as the graveyard of empires.

Sensing an opportunity to spring a trap for its Cold War foe, the US government would ensure that Afghanistan would become the Soviets' Vietnam. Via the CIA and with the help of Pakistan, the White House funded the arming, training and deployment of the *mujahideen*, tribal-based resistance fighters who would ultimately bleed out the Soviets. American money and arms flooded into Pakistan from where it would cross the border into Afghanistan — it was American foreign policy in action.

Money and arms were all very well, but the struggle required a constant source of recruits. Riding the wave of militant Islam evident in the Wahhabi fundamentalism emerging from Saudi Arabia, the CIA billed resistance against the Soviets as a *jihad*, a holy struggle against foreign crusaders. This attracted the attention of a host of interested foreigners, including a young Saudi student named Osama bin Laden. American taxpayer dollars, coupled with Saudi oil money, pushed this narrative into the tribal frontiers of Pakistan, where *madrassas*, religious schools dedicated to the recitation of the Quran, sprang up. Years later, these same *madrassas* would churn out the same warriors who would drag the Americans directly into another struggle in Afghanistan.

The American strategy worked and in 1989, ten years after they rolled into Kabul, the Soviets headed back across the Amu Darya River, leaving a trail of burnt tanks and trucks that became iconic symbols of Afghanistan. In the political vacuum left by the Soviets, the *mujahideen* leaders, previously united against a common enemy, now faced themselves. In 1992, the first bullets in Afghanistan's civil war were fired. Kabul, which had remained largely unscathed over the previous decades, was the scene of a brutal and bloody street battle between factions divided across sectarian and ethnic lines. This period in Afghan history is a tale of bloodletting the likes of which the country had never seen, exposing deep fault-lines in Afghan politics and society. Ethno-sectarian militias formed across the country, with urban centres like Kabul, Herat and Mazar-e-Sharif the most violent battlefields. It was not just a national crisis. Afghanistan became a battleground for its neighbours, particularly Shi'a Iran and Sunni Pakistan. No one escaped recrimination as internecine violence gripped the country. My father recalls this time as one of the darkest periods in his life.

As Afghanistan collapsed in on itself, a new force entered the realm. The Taliban (the Arabic word means entered the realm. The Taliban (the Arabic word means 'students'), emerged out of the *madrassas* with a hard-line religious fundamentalism that was etched into their minds through years of extremist doctrine. Ever since the fall of the Ottoman Empire in 1919, fundamentalist preachers had blamed the decline of the Islamic world on the moral decay of Muslim society. The Taliban believed that in order to make the Muslim world great again, it was necessary to revert to living life as it was at the time of the Prophet Muhammad. They would turn the clock back to the seventh century.

After taking the southern city of Kandahar in 1994 the Taliban stormed up the country, and by September 1996 they had claimed Kabul. They announced that the country had been reborn and would henceforth be known as the Islamic Emirate of Afghanistan.

The Taliban began creating the model Islamic society they believed would bring them closer to Allah. Women could not leave the house without a male chaperone. Any woman out and about without an all-covering burqa could be killed for blasphemy. Western influence was considered *haram*, sinful — music, television, radio, photos, books, cinemas and social gatherings were banned. Men were expected to grow full beards. Women and girls were forbidden from driving or attending school. The entire school curriculum was replaced with one text, the Quran.

were stoned in public. Murderers were executed by hanging or decapitation. Kabul's main stadium became an execution ground. The cruelty of the Taliban knew no bounds.

The Afghan exodus had begun with a trickle in the late 1970s as the Kabul elite and intelligentsia fled ahead of the anticipated communist coup. During the Soviet occupation the Afghan middle class hollowed out, the majority travelling as refugees to America or Europe. However, it was the civil war and the emergence of the Taliban that caused the most dramatic increase in refugees. Afghans of all backgrounds fled in their hundreds of thousands, crossing the border north into Tajikistan, west into Iran or east into Pakistan. Kabul, once home to over two million people, soon housed only half a million unfortunate souls who did not have the means to get out.

Like all fundamentalists, the Taliban dealt in absolutes. Hazara, being ethnically, linguistically, culturally and religiously different, represented a direct violation of the model Islamic society. The Taliban picked up where the Iron Emir had left off, waging a ferocious genocidal campaign to purify their Islamic Emirate. Following a defeat in Mazar-e-Sharif, partly due to Hazara militias, the Taliban retook the city in 1998. In an effort to avenge their defeat, Taliban leadership issued an edict that Hazara were *kafir*, infidels. Mazar-e-Sharif, a city built on old trading routes, saw its ancient streets run with blood, the majority of the victims being Hazara.

Although the persecution of Hazara had been in momentum since the beginning of the civil war, the edict gave Taliban forces the green light to wage genocide. Over two days, 5000–10,000 Hazara were executed in Mazar-e-Sharif, with thousands more taken prisoner or disappeared. Taliban would drive through the narrow city streets and, from the backs of their pickup trucks, shoot at random any man, woman or child they saw. In certain neighbourhoods they would barge into houses, slitting the throats of males before shooting the wives and daughters. Other men and boys were loaded into containers and taken into the desert, where they would be left to die of suffocation in the stifling heat.

The victims were left for days on end, baking in the sun until the stench became too much even for the Taliban. In Zabul province, the bodies of thousands of Hazara men, women and children who had gone missing were later discovered in mass graves. In May 2000 the bodies of 31 Hazara were discovered after being detained months earlier. In the Yakawlang district of Bamiyan the Taliban executed some 200 civilians on 8 January 2001. Bamiyan province, home to the Great Buddhas, also saw significant mass killings of Hazara families.

As well as the mass atrocities, random killings became a daily occurrence. After seizing an area, Taliban militants would establish a checkpoint and start to single out Hazara from buses and taxis. They would be beaten and robbed before being killed and left on the side of the road.

Exactly a century after the Iron Emir's conquest of Hazarajat, the Taliban, it seemed, had come to finish the job. The persecution of the Hazara continues today, with almost daily killings reported in Afghanistan and Pakistan.

The fall in 1998 of Mazar-e-Sharif and Bamiyan, the headquarters for the Hazara-based militias, marked a turning point in the war. Their militias splintered, leaving Hazara undefended against the brutality of the Taliban. A Taliban blockade was established around Hazarajat, crippling the already fragile economy by cutting off fuel, medical supplies and food. My father recalls how the price of everything went up as scarcity cut in. Clinics and pharmacy shelves were empty, and many people died as a result of preventable or curable ailments. Families went hungry as grain stores were rationed, then depleted, and the price of wheat went beyond reach. Animals were slaughtered as their owners could no longer afford to feed them. As news of each Taliban atrocity reached our village, it soon became clear that it was only a matter of time before they came for us.

It is amidst this violence and misery that our story begins.

4.

LEAVING THE
VALLEY

ASK ANY AFGHAN villager when they were born and they will most likely say 1 January. This is because most don't have a birth certificate. Many were home-birthed, and with the parents being illiterate, there are often no markers of a child's birth. As such, when arriving in a foreign country, parents do their best to provide a date that seems plausible. With little connection to the cities, and no newspapers, television or radio, they use local events to pinpoint the date of a birth, joining the dots from faded memory. Those who can't be bothered go with 1 January.

'Well, Ibrahim was born just before the harvest in which the Rahimis bought their horse. Zahir Shah was still the king at the time — I remember a traveller told me that.'

And so when I ask when I was born, Mum gives a similar answer.

'You were born just before the second harvest after Ali was born.'

It was sometime in the mid-1990s, according to both my parents. The neighbours had just bought a second cow, the Taliban had not yet emerged in Afghanistan, and the civil war in Kabul raged on.

I was number five in the Nazari clan, following Hussein, my eldest brother; Shekufah, my only sister; Sakhi, the middle child; and Ali, recently promoted to second-youngest. I was planned insofar as a subsistence farmer plans to have children to help in the fields.

'Another boy! You are so blessed!' exclaimed the other village women when I entered the world.

In a culture where sons are prized for their breadwinning ability, and daughters seen as a liability who needed to be married off, my birth continued Mum's lucky streak. I would be able to help Dad tend to the land and, God willing, would bring honour to the family.

My earliest memory as a child in Afghanistan is one that I cherish deeply. I was perhaps no more than three or four, watching Mum and Shekufah pull fresh naan out of the *tandoor*. The sun was setting, and Dad and the others would soon be home from the fields. Mum, sensing my eagerness to help, asked me to wrap the naan so they wouldn't get cold. Instead, I ripped off a corner of the warm bread, ran upstairs and climbed onto the roof, yelling at Dad that he'd better hurry home or I would eat the lot!

I was too young for school, and seeing my siblings get ready every morning made me jealous. One day, after I promised I'd be on my best behaviour, Mum agreed to let me walk with Ali and Sakhi to the local *masjid*, the gold-domed building that collected students from Sungjoy and surrounding villages. I sat cross-legged on the dirt floor, following the Arabic on the page as the teacher recited the Quran. While some kids are gifted with the slingshot, and others adept with a shovel, I found my strength in words. On my first day at school, as the teacher was mid-sentence, I piped up and pointed out that the double macron made an 'n' sound, something he'd overlooked when reciting the previous passage. The class burst out laughing at the five-year-old who had corrected the priest.

I immediately felt my face flush red, and anticipated a severe reprimand. Corporal punishment was common in Afghanistan, and knew no bounds. Minor incidents could be met with a slap to the face or a kick up the backside. Serious misdemeanours warranted a caning, usually with a fresh branch or a piece of industrial rope. I wondered what punishment the teacher had in mind for the unenrolled five-year-old who had called him out in public.

'Class, our newest student is correct. The *tanween fattha* indeed makes a *noon* sound,' he said, echoing my point before correcting the earlier passage and carrying on.

Although I was never officially enrolled, I tagged along with my brothers every day from then on. Thursday, the last day of class before the weekend, was assessment day. Lacking pen and paper, we would write on a wooden board using a bamboo stick dipped in ink. Once the teacher had seen our handwriting, we would spit on a piece of fabric and wipe away the ink before it dried. The high schools were slightly better equipped, with blackboards and chalk, but the instruction remained the same — students sitting cross-legged on the dirt floor while the teacher did their best to convey the basics of reading, writing and arithmetic.

Education has always been a central tenet of life in the highlands. Only dire necessity had forced my parents' generation to skip school. For children born in the middle of drought and poverty, education was a luxury their parents could not afford. Mum, the youngest of four children, lost her father to sickness when she was a child, leaving her and her siblings living with their mother in their tiny one-room hut.

Dad learnt to read and write as a teenager in Iran,

becoming one of the few local boys of his generation who were literate.

By the time we were born, things had improved significantly. Our upbringing, as primal and sparse as it may sound, was still brighter than Mum and Dad could ever have imagined as children themselves. We would all, including our sister, go to school and open our minds to a world that remained locked to them. Dad didn't expect us to become scholars, but hoped we would grow confident enough to one day venture beyond Sungjoy. His travels to Iran and the time spent on the road had opened his eyes to the world beyond the mountains. He hoped that in time we would be able to make the most of the opportunities that lay there.

Around the time I started school, the newest addition to the Nazari clan entered the world. Mum had always wanted another girl and had joked that she would stop having kids after she got one. Like most babies, this daughter entered the world crying, and she never stopped. The nurses and midwives at the little makeshift clinic in a nearby town could not work out why. She appeared physically healthy, but with no medical equipment to check for any internal issues, they were stumped. The hospitals in Kabul or Ghazni might have helped, but with war raging in the city streets, making that journey was a risk no one wanted to take. Mum brought her new baby home and did her best to soothe the fretful child. An elderly woman from another village was consulted. A witchdoctor of sorts, she rubbed milk into the baby's skin, burned incense, wrapped her in a blend of herbs and a length of fabric, but to no avail. After nine days in obvious agony, the baby passed away. Those days had been spent in such worry and distress, my parents never got around to giving her a name.

No parent should have to bury a child, but in Afghanistan, as in much of the developing world, infant mortality is shockingly high. It is a cruel fate that is thankfully now less prevalent, due to slowly improving access to medical care and rural education programmes.

The loss of her child rocked Mum deeply, but she did as she had always done: picked herself up and got on with life. Our parents' strength in the face of adversity is a pillar that has always held our family firm.

By 1999 the Taliban controlled more than 80 per cent of the country. The factions that had once fought one another had largely coalesced against this common foe, but after years of civil war and defections the resistance was crumbling. The Taliban were wresting control of more and more territory, and in time the conflict began to reach the highlands. Up to this point we had been sheltered by the mountainous terrain from the worst of the violence. But after taking Ghazni, the provincial capital, the Taliban set their sights on the rest of the province. Ghazni province is crucially located between Kabul and the southern provinces from which the Taliban drew their strength. Establishing control of this area was of strategic importance to the Taliban in their mission to make Islam great again.

One by one, towns like ours began falling to the Taliban as they came closer and closer to Sungjoy. Armed with ancient long guns and antique hunting rifles, locals formed militias as they had done against the Iron Emir. But the Taliban only needed to wait as internal conflict and a shortage of ammunition slowly crippled the resistance. With no central government, the Afghan National Army was in complete disarray at this point. The few who had not been killed or injured or defected to a local militia had split into regional factions, barely containing the fighting near their own bases.

There would be no help from elsewhere.

With an intermittent radio signal being Sungjoy's only connection to the world beyond the mountains, Dad became the most reliable source of news for our village because he regularly travelled around making deliveries. After he returned home from a run, the men of the village would gather in the courtyard of our home to hear the news.

'The Taliban are close. It won't be long now.'

'What should we do? We don't have anything to fight with!'

It was true. Sungjoy was positioned higher up the mountain than the other villages. The isolation had served us well in the past, offering relative safety for decades. There were no forts, no checkpoints, not even a prison for miles. The downside to this peaceful existence was now becoming clear: no one was ready for when the war arrived, and there was no one nearby to help.

On his runs Dad had seen a steady flow of people – on foot, on horseback and on carts – fleeing their villages.

'I've seen many houses boarded up. Entire villages have emptied. I don't know where they are going, but perhaps it is a safer bet than staying.'

Internally displaced peoples – those who lack the means to escape the country – are the unseen face of any refugee crisis. For those Afghans who could not travel far to escape the Taliban, the northern province of Badakhshan offered some hope. By the start of 2000 it was the only Afghan province not under Taliban control. Badakhshan was controlled by the Northern Alliance, a collection of *mujahideen* who had united under Ahmad Shah Massoud, a charismatic guerrilla leader who offered the last hope for a return to stability.

'How can we walk away? We have lived on this land for generations. If we leave, who will take care of our land and our animals? There will be nothing to come back to!'

The conversation become more animated, more desperate.

'And if we *don't* leave, there will be nothing left of us! You heard how they slaughtered those poor families in Mazar-e-Sharif and left their bodies to be eaten by dogs. You think the Talibs will be merciful to us?'

'Leave and go where? I'd rather die here than be killed on the side of the road.'

'Brothers, think of your families. What life will they live if you go to the front lines and get killed? Do you imagine the Taliban will let them tend to your lands? No, they will rape your wives and daughters and slit the throats of your sons.'

To stay or to go? The dilemma plagued people's minds, the only topic of conversation at Friday prayers. It hung in the valley like a bad smell, dominating every aspect of life. As summer turned to autumn, people were still considering their options.

We children knew mercifully little of this. Then one day, while walking home from school, I noticed a man nailing boards across his windows. His two sons were in our class and they had not been at school that day.

'You won't let in much light using wooden curtains!' Ali and I laughed.

'I don't think there is much light left in Sungjoy. Every day it gets darker.'

Ali and I looked at the clear blue sky and shrugged, not understanding what he meant.

Later that night Dad explained that there was a war raging in the distance, and that these people wanted to escape the violence. But he told us in such a way as to not scare us. How do you explain war to a child?

Dad said the man and his family would be gone by the morning. True enough, the next morning there was no trace of them. Boards had been placed across all the windows. There were no shoes at the front door, which had two large beams nailed across it. The only thing left behind was the little straw broom used for sweeping the courtyard. A friend had picked them up before sunrise and driven them beyond the mountains.

As winter approached, more and more houses were boarded up. Where once our morning walk to school had been a joyous time in which we met up and played with other village kids, Ali and I soon found ourselves alone, walking through a valley of ghost houses.

THE FIRST SNOW of the winter fell across the valley and Dad knew it was time. My eldest brother Hussein, at fifteen, had just finished high school. In normal times he might have got married and helped Dad expand the trucking business. But these were not normal times. A boy of fifteen was a perfect recruit for the local militias who were constantly urging each village to provide reinforcements to bolster their depleting ranks. Hussein would be a sacrificial lamb. Or if he became a driver he would be picked off by the Taliban; any military-aged Hazara posed a threat.

Seeing his eldest son's life in the balance, Dad decided it was best for Hussein to go to Iran. Dad himself had not been there for over a decade but he knew some former colleagues who would offer Hussein a place to stay. He must leave before the roads became impassable.

Hussein did not protest. He knew it fell on him to shoulder the weight of Dad's hopes.

I don't remember saying goodbye to my big brother. I had learnt to walk as he held my hands, and I had explored Sungjoy as a toddler on Hussein's shoulders.

The next morning he was gone. Seeing his blanket folded up next to mine, I wondered if I would ever see him again.

Hussein's departure for Iran nearly broke our mother,

but she did not have much time to process it before she found she was pregnant again. Having said goodbye to one son, Mum gave birth to another. Blond, and premature, Mojtaba was born as winter gave way to spring in 2000. It was a ray of sunshine amidst a brewing storm.

A YEAR LATER we were sitting at dinner one night when Dad announced the news that would change our lives forever.

'We are leaving. We cannot stay here any more.'

There was a deafening silence as his words hung in the air.

It was not a surprise. It was the spring of 2001 and the Taliban were firmly in charge of Afghanistan. They had just destroyed the great Buddhas of Bamiyan and set about massacring the Hazara living under their shadow.

By then, more than half of the homes in Sungjoy had been boarded up and abandoned. Our once thriving village was dying, as if felled by a deadly blight. Every day we noticed more classmates absent. Worse, some nights we could hear the thunder of automatic gunfire from the valleys close by, shattering the tranquility we had once known. As every day passed, death crept closer.

'Abdul, I know others have left, but how can we follow

them? Mojtaba cannot even walk,' said Mum, breaking the silence at last.

'If we stay, he won't even be able to breathe much longer.'

Dad's reply punctured the air, as if his truck had rammed into the house.

'I have had passports made for all of us. I did it on a recent trip to Kabul. A man will come and take my truck tomorrow. He will pay me cash, and we will use that to get us out of here.'

We were shocked. Dad had clearly been planning this for a while. He had passports, and on his most recent run to Kabul he said he had procured visas.

'Visas? To where?' asked Sakhi.

'Pakistan. I have an old friend in Quetta. I rang him from Kabul and he has offered us a place to stay while we get back on our feet.'

None of us had been to Pakistan. All we knew was that it was the country next door – and it was where the Taliban came from. We sat in silence trying to take it all in.

'Tomorrow will be your last day of school. You will say goodbye and come home immediately. We will not be leaving in the dark. We will leave tomorrow afternoon.'

We went to bed that evening for our final night in Sungjoy, our last in the life we knew.

Tomorrow would be a new dawn.

5.

NEVER LOOK BACK

WE LEFT SUNGJOY at midday. That morning we went to the school to say goodbye to our teachers. Mum had baked some naan the night before and I handed it to the principal as we told him the news. He was not surprised. He had contemplated leaving as well, perhaps taking a job in one of the refugee schools in Iran or Pakistan, but his heart was in the highlands.

When we got home our lorry was gone, and Mum and Dad had a couple of duffel bags and one large trunk stacked neatly by the front door. It looked as if Mum had been crying for most of the morning, but Dad remained stoic as ever. He had made the best decision he could for his family; the rest was in God's hands.

I climbed onto the roof to take in one last view of the valley. Spring was in the air, and the valley seemed to have received a fresh coat of paint after a cold winter. I could see ghost houses dotting the hillsides, and an eerie silence cloaked the valley. There were few children left, and the large flocks of sheep that roamed the hillsides had been sold to traders. The only sound was the creek winding its way through the fields.

As I climbed down I saw a blue lorry with a trailer emerge from behind a hill. It was a friend of Dad's who was on his way to Ghazni, carrying a load of generators and other industrial equipment. It stopped by the creek and we walked down the hill towards it. The driver had reserved a space in the trailer beside the stack of generators for us to sit and be concealed.

'Don't say a word, okay? I'll knock twice on this window when we're in the clear,' the driver whispered to us from the cabin.

We sat in the trailer concealed by boxes and blankets as the lorry grunted along the dirt road. My last image of Sungjoy was of the slender silver creek shining amidst a cloud of dust.

It was a silent trip as we contemplated what life had in store for us. Our family had called Sungjoy home for nearly a century, since the days when my great-grandparents had settled there, and we were one of the most prominent households. Would we ever come back? Would we climb those hills, swim in the water, or breathe the fresh air ever again?

Dust and diesel fumes choked us as the truck hummed and whirred along the dirt road for hours. Mum muffled Mojtaba's cries with a corner of her headscarf. I couldn't tell how long we had been there but through a slit in the fabric I could see it was beginning to get dark. As the sun set, the old lorry sliced through the darkness with its faded headlights.

Close to midnight we arrived at the first stop on our journey. The village of Dawoud is a pitstop for travellers going to Anguri. Dad had an acquaintance who lived on the outskirts of Dawoud. He did not know we were coming, but we relied on the ancient Afghan custom of opening the door to any guest. Luckily, he was home, and sure enough, he offered us some *chai qud naan* (tea and bread) before laying out some mattresses on the floor. We were so tired that we all went straight to bed, laying our heads down to rest in a foreign place for the first time in our lives.

It seemed like hardly any time later that I was being shaken awake. Mum was bent over me, whispering that it was time to go. It was still dark out and the roosters had not yet woken. Another lorry was due any minute and we had no time to spare. As I folded my blankets the lorry appeared, the driver flashing a torch in the cabin to signal his arrival. Dad slipped some folded notes underneath his pillow before he led us out of the house. We climbed up on the back of the lorry but the driver insisted that Dad sit in the cabin, so it would look as if they were a tandem team. I sat on Dad's lap as the driver put his foot down and the lorry pulled away, leaving a trail of dust.

As we slipped between hills and valleys, the beauty of Ghazni province presented itself like a flower blooming in the morning sun. To many, the name Afghanistan conjures up images of barren deserts and desolate plains. While this is true for the southern provinces, much of the country is a bucolic blend of soaring peaks and fertile valleys dotted with productive villages.

Our lorry coursed its way through valleys, following rivers and streams that had carved their way through the mountains. Snow-capped mountains soared high into the crisp blue sky as we motored along through orchards and wheatfields.

While I was drinking in the beauty that lay beyond Sungjoy, the rest of the family hiding in the back of the lorry were in a bad way. Wedged among a mass of boxes, ropes and other industrial equipment, they had all become carsick, particularly Shekufah. Severely dehydrated after vomiting, she looked awful, but we could not stop for fear of being ambushed by bandits.

Eventually we reached the small town of Qalat, not much more than an intersection consisting of a petrol station, a couple of shops and a restaurant. The lorry driver parked behind some trees and ushered us out quietly one by one. Mum laid out a blanket by some trees and unwrapped some fresh *bosragh* and *bolani*, fried bread and stuffed flat bread, which our hosts had given her the night before. It was odd — we were picnicking by a peaceful stream in the middle of a war zone.

Shekufah couldn't eat and, even though we were on stable ground, continued to vomit. The mix of motion sickness, diesel fumes and claustrophobia had rendered her a pale-faced ghost. Dad had spotted a pharmacy by the petrol station and piggybacked his only daughter down the road. Dad recalls today how the pharmacist injected her with a saline solution through her clothes.

We had already packed by the time they returned. Dad and I resumed our seat in the cabin and we were soon back on the road.

The road to Kandahar is one of the most dangerous in the country, if not the world. The southern provinces of Afghanistan had long been a lawless stretch of desert dominated by bandits and tribal militias; killings, kidnappings and robberies were common. It was also the Taliban heartland. There would be no stops and the family were to remain hidden for the entire journey.

I gripped Dad's hand as the lorry gained speed. The Ghazni–Kandahar highway was the first stretch of asphalt-covered road I had been on. It stretched out like a black serpent sunning itself in the desert. The driver's knuckles turned white as the lorry rode the serpent into the horizon. The road was eerily empty, save for the burnt-out bodies of trucks and tanks, many of which were from the Soviet war. Our lorry crept past the desolation as if we were astronauts exploring the Martian landscape.

We reached Kandahar after dark and settled into a one-room travel inn that Dad remembered from a trip he had made to the city many years ago. Exhausted from two days of rough travelling, we crashed out immediately for our second night away from home.

'Tomorrow I will find us someone who can take us across the border. Today was dangerous but the border crossing will be even more risky. Everyone needs to stay calm and have faith.' Dad projected calm but I could tell he was uneasy. The journey to this point had gone smoothly, but plenty more challenges lay ahead. We said nothing. What could we say? We were about to leave the country we had known all our lives on a journey with no end in sight.

I woke up early the next day and followed some of the guests at the inn who had climbed on the roof to pray. I looked out over the ancient city. Kandahar is home to one of the oldest known human settlements, with some buildings dating back to 1000 BC. As a major trading city, it had seen epochal transformations as different empires rose and fell. Now, it bore the scars of the most recent change. Many of the buildings were riddled with bullet holes, and there were mountains of rubble where once stood shops and homes. An electric unease hung in the air, as if anything still alive was holding its breath.

'Get down from the roof!' Dad had seen me from the street and motioned me to get inside.

'I've found a driver who will take us to Quetta.' Dad seemed excited. 'Let's keep faith.'

'Inshallah,' whispered Mum under her breath. God willing indeed.

A beat-up *saraacha* — the ubiquitous Toyota station-wagon that had replaced donkey and cart in most cities — pulled up a few moments later. We piled in, and the driver sped through the city.

'It's best to get there earlier in the day,' he said. 'The guards lose patience as the day warms up. The sun fries their brains.'

He was a young man. Ferrying people and goods across the border was as lucrative as it was dangerous, and in a country with few prospects, young men did what they could to put food on the table. An Arabic scroll bearing the traveller's prayer hung from the rear-view mirror.

Crammed in the back seat, I gazed out the window as we left the city behind. Along the road I witnessed a horde of other families fleeing the ravages of war. They were mostly walking or sitting on donkey-drawn carts, clutching an assortment of colourful bags. A few were riding camels. We were all headed to the border.

Spin Boldak is a filthy, dusty border town that reeked of animal waste and sweat. We arrived in the late morning to find a throng of refugees all vying to cross the border into Pakistan.

With most colonial-era borders, the lines on a map rarely align with reality on the ground. The Durand Line was no exception. It was the result of an agreement between Sir Mortimer Durand, a secretary of the British Indian government, and the Iron Emir. The agreement, signed in 1893, formally separated British India (later partitioned into India and Pakistan) from Afghanistan. The agreement split traditional Pashtun and Punjabi areas down the middle, so nomadic tribes and farmers continued to live as if the colonial cartographers had run out of ink when it came to drawing Afghanistan's borders. The Taliban now controlled the checkpoint, but they were reluctant to alienate their fellow Pashtuns and Punjabis by enforcing restrictions on their movement. As far as the Taliban were concerned, the more refugees leaving Afghanistan the better, for it meant bullets could be saved for their mission to purge the Islamic Emirate of infidels.

As the *saraacha* crept through the streets of Spin Boldak the trickle of refugees ballooned into a vocal throng, with shouting and scuffling as camels, carts and cars jockeyed for position. Closer to the checkpoint, the Taliban presence grew heavier. The armed militants pacing the area were dressed in the traditional black robes, with a turban concealing most of their faces. The men processing documents had their weapon of choice, an AK-47, strapped to their back, while the rest had theirs at the waist, ready to fire.

Our car eventually neared the final barrier, a large metal pole wrapped in barbed wire that was blocking the road, with militants standing by. An observation tower had been erected on either side of the road, each housing another half a dozen or so Taliban gunmen. Large boulders had been spaced out around the area so that anyone who tried to run would be forced to zigzag and be an easy target.

As the queue ahead of us continued to thin, our hearts

beat louder and louder. There was a commotion ahead. The car immediately in front of us had been directed to pull aside rather than stop. We couldn't make out the Pashto, but it was clear the gunman wasn't happy with the driver. He opened the door and pulled the driver out of his seat. Before the man could protest, the gunman raised the butt of his rifle and brought it down on the driver's head, knocking him out cold. A child screamed from the car before the gunman dealt another blow to the unconscious man, now bleeding profusely from one ear.

As the gunman went for a third strike, a senior commander shouted from his post. He was tall and big-bellied, with his entire body from the neck down swathed in a big khaki shawl. A black turban wrapped his head, with one end hanging loosely down his side. He barked an order for the militant to leave, then approached the man on the ground and nudged him with the toe of his boot. The commander leaned inside the car and ordered two teenage boys to collect the driver and put him in their car and turn around. They would not be going to Pakistan today.

The commander then approached our car. From up close I could see his bulging bloodshot eyes and caught the stench of sweat and *naswar*, a pungent powdered tobacco. He gestured for Dad and our driver to step out of the *saraacha*. I felt hot tears roll down my cheeks as I thought about Dad being felled by a blow to the head. The commander escorted the men to his post, a wooden shed with a cracked window facing us. I saw Dad and the driver talking profusely, proffering passports and visas.

Dad later told us it became clear there was nothing wrong with our documents but the commander wanted money. Dad reached into his jacket pocket and pulled out an envelope with some cash. The commander snatched the envelope and it disappeared under his shawl. For a family of our size, apparently it wasn't enough. He eyed Dad's hands. On his wedding finger was an old silver ring with a bright blue *noqra*, a lapis lazuli, and he wore a watch on the other hand. Without being told, Dad handed the commander both heirlooms. A curt nod and we were on our way.

Every minute they were in the shed had felt like a lifetime. A wave of relief swept through the car as Dad and the driver got back in their seats. But as the engine roared, the commander came back out of the shed.

'Not so fast!' he barked.

Hearts in our throats, we wondered what cruelty he would inflict on us now.

He leaned his elbow on the driver-side window, the other hand resting on the butt of his rifle. He eyed Dad's beard and asked him to place his fist under his chin. A full beard should come out under the fist. Dad's was short.

Our Central Asian genetics gave us many things, but thick beard growth wasn't one of them.

'You must model yourself on the Prophet.'

'Alhamdulillah,' said my father. By the grace of God.

That seemed to be the right answer. The commander stood up and walked away. Without a second's hesitation our driver pressed the accelerator, navigating around the barbed wire and zigzagging past the boulders.

Afghanistan disappeared in a cloud of dust behind us.

6.

ROLLING
THE DICE

ENTERING PAKISTAN WENT much more smoothly. The border guards were used to refugees, and appreciated those who had their documents in order. As always, bribes accelerated the processing time significantly. After a series of payments, we were in Pakistan.

The driver suggested we break the journey at the border town of Chaman, but Dad insisted we put as much distance as possible between us and the Taliban. We drove for the rest of the day, racing ahead as if we were being chased by some wild animal. From Chaman, the desert gave way to rock as we climbed higher. The road to Quetta was cut into the side of a mountain, with a vertigo-inducing drop down one side. The little *saraacha* crept along, tyres clinging to the asphalt as hard as I was gripping Dad's arm. One misjudgement and the car could plunge hundreds of metres into the river below.

The mountain pass seemed to go on forever, and by the time we began to come down the other side we were all throwing up into plastic bags. We arrived in Quetta just before sunset. To our relief, the roads were smooth again and the vomiting stopped — not that there was much left to bring up.

QUETTA IS HOME to about a million people, and is the capital of Pakistan's Balochistan province. The city has a sizeable Afghan population, which began with Hazara refugees escaping the Iron Emir. Later, Afghans of all backgrounds sought refuge from the Soviet invasion and the ensuing civil war. By the time we arrived, in April 2001, Pakistan was home to more than two million registered Afghan refugees, the vast majority of whom had fled the Taliban. A further two million Afghans were living in Pakistan as undocumented non-citizens.

At the time there were more than 150 refugee camps in Pakistan, most of which were dotted along the border. Many Afghans had settled in refugee camps and informal settlements in and around the cities of

Quetta, Karachi and Peshawar. The biggest of these, and the most prominent symbol of the Afghan refugee flow into Pakistan, was the Shamshato Refugee Camp on the outskirts of Peshawar. The 50,000 residents of Shamshato, like most refugees in camps, lived in squalid conditions, eating and sleeping next to open sewer lines and with no access to clean water or electricity.

They survived on the generosity of foreign aid and their own spirit and resolve. Then as now, refugees would queue for hours for their daily rations of bread and cooking oil, made available through the United Nations World Food Program and agencies such as the United States Agency for International Development. For millions of refugees around the world, camps such as Shamshato present a tiny bubble of hope, security and reprieve from the hunger, violence and poverty they have endured to get there.

Refugee camps are supposed to be a temporary solution but unfortunately, as conflicts continue to break out and evolve, many become permanent semi-official enclaves — cities in themselves. Shamshato, and other prominent refugee camps such as Dadaab in Kenya, Kutupalong in Bangladesh, and Zaatari in Jordan, stand as permanent monuments to the conflicts which ravage populations and upend lives.

Although such camps are the most visible embodiment

of the refugee experience, three-quarters of refugees live outside the camps, housed with relatives or in private accommodation, where they are afforded the luxuries of running water and some privacy. Dad had a contact in Quetta, a man he had worked with at the Timber Factory decades ago. He had called him from Kandahar and said if we were successful, we would arrive in Quetta by nightfall.

The Gold Hajji, so called because he had a gold tooth implant, had laboured with Dad in Iran 30 years earlier. He had returned to Afghanistan a month before the communist coup d'état in 1978. Sensing the imminent conflict, he had left Kabul again, this time for Pakistan, where he eventually settled in Quetta. He had built a life for himself there, setting up a small corner store catering to the growing Afghan community.

The Gold Hajji was one of the earliest proponents of Hazara Town, a private settlement on the outskirts of Quetta that was home to some 70,000 Afghans, the majority of whom were Hazara. From all over the city, Hazara refugees who had been living in informal settlements or in *masjid*, or sleeping on the streets, moved to Hazara Town, attracted by the relative security, and the opportunities for education and jobs. The settlement burgeoned, with schools, shops, homes and livelihoods. Children attended school, while men worked as labourers, miners, textile workers or shopkeepers. The few women who decided to work outside the home took up embroidery, carpet weaving or quilt making, while those who were better educated became teachers. Hazara Town was a replica of life in a typical town in Hazarajat.

Our driver dropped us off in front of a mud-brick wall in an alleyway of Hazara Town. The Gold Hajji opened his door as we unloaded our bags and bid the driver goodbye. Our host was a short, plump man with a broad smile. His wife and children gathered around him and between them they rolled out the welcome mat as if we were distant relatives.

'Abdul! How many decades has it been?' He embraced Dad as if they were long-lost brothers.

We were ushered inside as the sun was setting. The Gold Hajji had prepared his guesthouse for our arrival, and after three days on the road we were immensely grateful. As Dad and the Gold Hajji chatted about our journey, we were served a platter of fruit to ease our empty tummies. It was an eclectic mix of strange fruits I had not seen before. One that caught my eye was a large oval in beautiful shades of orange, red and pink. Sakhi told me this was a mango. By now my eyes were fixated on another exotic specimen – a long, curved yellow bow joined to other yellow bows at the end in a bunch. I pulled one off and bit into it. The skin was tough and didn't chew well. I put the strange fruit down and the Gold Hajji erupted in laughter.

'A true boy of the highlands! These are not *chukree*, these are *kela* — you have to peel the skin off first.' He demonstrated how to clip the top and unfurl the peel to get at the soft, sweet banana flesh.

I went to bed that night in a foreign land, with a tummy full of exotic fruit.

WE ALL SLEPT in the next day, our bodies luxuriating in the soft blankets. Dad and the Gold Hajji had stayed up late discussing our next steps, and Dad briefed us on their conversation.

'We will stay here for the next few days, maybe a week or so, until we decide what to do next. The way I see it, there are three options. We could register for a tent at the nearest refugee camp, find a place to rent in Hazara Town, or move somewhere else in Pakistan.'

We chewed our naan and sipped our *chai*. Dad had planned to get us out of immediate danger, and he had succeeded. But did we have to keep moving? At every juncture, Dad had asked what was best for his family, and that touchstone had steered his every decision. Now he explained that Hazara Town was a short respite from the violence of Afghanistan, but it was not a final stop.

Hazara have been living in Quetta for over a century. Never welcome in Pakistan, they have faced rising anti-Afghan (and particularly anti-Shi'a) sentiments. The Taliban and their sympathisers routinely kidnapped or killed any Hazara they found outside the barbed-wire gates of Hazara Town. We had been sitting ducks in Hazarajat, and now we were sitting ducks in the largest and poorest province of Pakistan.

Although the situation was dangerous in 2001, it has reached boiling point in recent years. A plethora of terror groups — including Al Qaeda affiliates, the Taliban, Lashkar-e-Jangvi and the Islamic State (IS) — have waged a bloody campaign against the Hazara of Quetta. Bomb blasts regularly tear through Hazara Town. Labourers are gunned down on their way home or at their worksites. Hazara disappear without trace, only for their bodies to be discovered on the roadside days later. As this book was being written, there were still numerous deadly attacks against the Hazara of Quetta. The most sickening to date involved eleven Hazara coalminers who were kidnapped from their worksite in January 2021 by IS militants. The miners had their throats slit and their bodies dumped on the roadside.

WHAT COULD WE do? The refugee camps were filthy, overcrowded and no place for a family of our size, especially with a newborn. Our parents had no other contacts in Pakistan.

'There is one other option,' said Dad, 'but I need to talk to some people.'

'What option?' asked Mum.

'It's not worth talking about when I don't even know if it's possible.'

'What are you talking about?' Mum didn't want to wait for an answer. 'Going to Iran?'

'No, a little further. Forget about it for now. It's probably beyond us anyway.'

We were all curious, but we were interrupted by the Gold Hajji.

'Do you want to see your neighbourhood?' he asked. We were all eager to stretch our legs after three days of being boxed up.

We walked out of the Hajji's house and down the alleyway. The Gold Hajji pointed out the local school, the *masjid*, the market, and the patch of dirt where all the children gathered to play football, cricket and volleyball. Quetta was the first major city I had ever seen and it was overwhelming — a raging torrent of people and commerce a million miles from the tranquil serenity of Sungjoy. Life all in a rush, like the stream after the winter snow had melted. The air smelled of wood smoke, sewage, sweat and decomposing trash. After a few minutes my skin was caked in a thick layer of dust.

DAYS TURNED TO weeks in the Gold Hajji's guesthouse as our parents tried to work out what to do next. Not wanting us to fall behind in our education, and with no decision on our next move, Dad was adamant that we resume our studies. Apart from a couple of months of tagging along with Ali and Sakhi to school in Sungjoy, my first official classroom learning took place in a little primary school down an alleyway in Hazara Town. Unlike the *masjid* in Sungjoy where we sat on the floor, this one had desks, chairs and a blackboard. We spent much of the day reciting passages from the Quran. I always found it odd as a Farsi speaker to read aloud in Arabic with little or no understanding of the words. It was rote learning — reciting a foreign language — and I found the recitations boring and meaningless. However, although I didn't understand Arabic, I developed impressive handwriting. I could write cursive script, linking the letters with fluidity like a master calligrapher. Years later when I started primary school again, in a faraway country, I was delighted to see my handwriting skills translated to the English alphabet as well.

Dad would complement our classes by bringing home strips of newspaper for us to read, eager to give us every opportunity he was denied as a child. One day he brought home a thick, colourful book with beautiful pictures — an atlas of the world. He pointed to Ghazni and traced our journey to Quetta. Little did I know, sitting in the corner of a guesthouse in Pakistan and browsing through the pages of the atlas, that our journey would cover half the globe before we would find home again.

Life in Quetta passed quickly. Ali and Sakhi took a liking to football and both quickly earned a reputation for having a deadly right foot. But as much as we loved playing football, we never stayed out after sunset for fear of being kidnapped by human traffickers. There had been a spate of disappearances, thought to be the work of underworld figures involved in organ harvesting, or sometimes holding people for ransom. The kidnap-for-ransom business preyed on schoolchildren.

Through school and football we became friends with lots of other refugee kids. Although many had arrived before us, and some had even been born in Quetta after their families had fled, we all shared the same experience of family flight from danger and desperation.

One evening, as Ali and I were flicking through the atlas after dinner, Dad broke the news.

'We are going to Australia,' he said bluntly.

As always, there was a silence.

'There's no future for us here. I've heard talk of some people who have made it to Australia by paying some people to take them there. It's our best shot.'

'How do we get there?' asked Mum incredulously. 'Australia is on the other side of the world!'

'We will fly, and then take a boat. I don't know the details yet, but it's what everyone is talking about.'

None of us had been on either an aeroplane or a boat before. Having spent a lifetime in the landlocked mountains, we were excited and simultaneously terrified at the prospect of navigating sky and sea.

'There are a few men meeting tomorrow to discuss whether it's actually possible. I'll go along and we can talk about it at dinner tomorrow night.'

Later that night, Shekufah and Sakhi came over to look at the atlas.

'Where is this place that Dad wants to go?' asked Shekufah.

I flicked through the pages to find the map of the globe and pointed to the large continent near the bottom surrounded by oceans.

'And where are we?' she asked, as Sakhi peered over her shoulder.

'Here!' I said, remembering what Dad had showed me on the first day.

'I don't understand how this picture works, but that looks very far to me.'

7.

ON THE ROAD AGAIN

WEEKS WENT BY with no word on what might happen next. Every day more and more refugees flooded into Quetta, overwhelming the little housing and few social services available. By June 2001 the Taliban had well and truly established themselves as the dominant power in Afghanistan. Millions of Afghans were displaced internally, and millions more had swarmed into Iran and Pakistan.

We had been living in Quetta for almost three months when Dad came home one night later than usual, and accompanied by a group of men.

'It is agreed: we will go to Australia. There is someone who will take us. And we won't be alone — these brothers will be joining us,' said Dad as he introduced the other men. They were all fathers and sons, some of whom had fled with their families to Quetta, like us, and others who had ventured solo.

They spoke of how they had hoped to be resettled overseas through the United Nations High Commissioner for Refugees (UNHCR), but that hope resembled more fantasy than reality. Globally, the UNHCR reports that less than 1 per cent of refugees are successful in their resettlement application to that organisation, a figure that has barely changed over the last two decades. This leaves the majority of refugees lost in a never-ending limbo. At the current rate of acceptances it would take centuries to clear the backlog of applicants.

After years in Quetta, these men believed Australia was their last hope. One of them had lost both parents in the massacre in Mazar-e-Sharif. He had fled with his pregnant wife to the highlands, where he left his family with a relative before setting off for Pakistan. He had hoped that after presenting his story to the UNHCR he might be resettled overseas, but he was still waiting after three years and felt he had no other choice. His newborn son had died of typhoid before he even had a chance to meet him.

Another man spoke of how his father had been killed

fighting in the local militia, and as the eldest son it was up to him to chart a path for his mother and siblings. Each story was more harrowing than the one before. Here were men, young and old, fathers and sons, who had left their families in search of a lifeline, and they had hit the end of the road.

They had heard rumours of refugees who had made it to Australia by boat. The most common path was to find a smuggler who could get them to Indonesia, and then another who would put them on a boat to Australia. All for the right price, of course. No one knew personally of anyone who had made the trek, but rumours abounded that there had been a number of successful journeys in recent years.

What the refugees were counting on was the international legal principle of 'non-refoulement'. Enshrined in the 1951 Convention Relating to the Status of Refugees, non-refoulement explicitly prohibits any signatory to the convention from expelling or returning a refugee 'to the frontiers of territories where his life or freedom would be threatened'. The thousands of refugees who arrived by boat or overland to foreign countries were counting on the host country to hear their claims for asylum and give them a chance.

It sounded simple, but Australia was so far away. Yet

these men were determined. After all they had sacrificed, they were willing to go one step further. What did they have to lose?

'I will find an agent,' said one of the men. 'Someone who can get us there safely.'

'I am eager to go as well, but you know I have little money,' said another. 'Please negotiate as best you can.'

'We need one who can promise us safe passage. I don't want to pay the ultimate price . . .'

As we children went to bed the room still buzzed with conversation. Everyone seemed excited by the prospect of a new life, but under the surface I could tell they were all uneasy.

THE NEXT FEW weeks were spent searching for an agent who could pave the way for us to board a flight to the Indonesian capital of Jakarta. We could not just buy tickets like ordinary passengers: we were Afghani refugees. No country would willingly admit such desperate people to even board a flight, let alone leave the airport if they got that far. People-smugglers worked the system by planting and paying off immigration and travel officials every step of the way.

Meanwhile, our group of friends seemed to swell by

the day as Hazara Town absorbed more and more refugees. One day after school, as Ali and I prepared to walk home, we saw Dad standing at the gate.

'Let's say goodbye to your teachers. You will not see them again.'

Here we were again. Although I had been at this school for only a few months, I was sad to say goodbye. I had developed a deep love of learning. Would I ever sit in a classroom again?

We got home to see that Mum had already packed our bags. Dad was pacing up and down the alleyway nervously. An agent had been found some weeks earlier and he had promised that when the time was right, Dad and the other men would receive a call. After we had left for school that morning, the call had come. A van would pick us up at three o'clock and take us to the bus depot.

It was now four o'clock and there was no sign of a van. Was it because of Quetta's unruly traffic, or had the agent run away with our money? Our normally calm father was clearly stressed. He had spent his life savings on this new venture. Now his pockets were empty and there was no sign of the van. After almost three months we had outstayed our welcome at the guesthouse and if we did not leave tonight as planned, we would soon be on the streets.

Four o'clock became five o'clock became six o'clock.

We stood in the courtyard, bags in hand, as the late afternoon sun began to set. Mum unwrapped some of the naan she had packed for the trip. As we bit into it, the screech of tyres pierced the quiet evening. The van had arrived.

A young dark-skinned Pakistani man, perhaps no older than twenty, opened the side door.

'Nazari?' he asked.

'Yes,' answered Dad.

'How many?'

'Including me, six.'

'I count seven,' said the man, pointing at Mojtaba, who was wrapped in a blanket under Mum's shawl.

'The baby is not even a year old. He can barely walk. He will remain in his mother's lap.'

'You paid for six!' hissed the man, the veins in his neck bulging.

'I will not leave my child here. We are one family and we will all be going.'

'Brother, I am just the driver. I have been told to pick up six people.'

'The baby is coming too. He will hide under the mother's chador. You won't even know he's there.'

The driver hesitated. He no doubt worked for some uncompromising people and wondered what would happen if he allowed a stowaway. But he was running late, and didn't want to delay further by calling his bosses.

'Not a word,' he said, before opening the door.

We piled in, and before we could sit down the van hurtled down the alleyway into the dark Quetta night.

8.

NAVIGATING SKY AND SEA

THE VAN SCREECHED into the bus depot on the outskirts of Quetta just before 10 p.m. Unlike Afghanistan, Pakistan was connected by an intercity bus system, and there were dozens of buses parked in rows, each displaying a different destination: Karachi, Islamabad, Lahore. The driver parked on the kerb and hurried us out.

'We're late. Get your bags and follow me. Quickly.'

We gathered ourselves and ran after the man, who was jogging awkwardly, seeming to inspect the underside of each bus. We arrived at a group of buses headed for Karachi.

'There, that one, with the white strip around the number plate. That's yours. Hurry.'

'Karachi?' asked Dad.

'Yes. Overnight to Karachi. You'll get there by the morning. After that, someone else will be in touch.'

Dad did not know if we could trust the man, and it wasn't as if we had receipts. Perhaps the agent had booked a one-way ticket to the furthest city in Pakistan to get rid of us, knowing it would be impossible for us ever to find him again.

The young man sensed Dad's hesitation.

'We are honourable people,' he said in his most reassuring tone. 'Get on. Your friends are already aboard.'

We had not noticed that the bus was full. It stood idling, lights off, curtains fully drawn. We walked towards the front of the bus and the door opened. Dad peered inside and recognised a man from his group sitting near the front with his family. By the time Dad turned to motion us on, the van driver had disappeared.

We took the remaining empty seats in the front. It seemed everyone had been waiting for us because there was a collective sigh of relief as the door closed and the bus began to move. I recognised some of the families from Quetta.

Ali and I were surrounded by luggage — above, below and beside us. It actually made for quite a comfortable setup and we both soon fell asleep.

The road from Quetta to Karachi is a 700-kilometre

stretch through mountain passes, desert and lush jungle. Much of it was spent in darkness as our bus stalked the highway with its load of illicit goods. To the untrained eye we were a busload of tourists, but to keen police officers we would stand out as desperate refugees to be squeezed for cash. The driver avoided stops for this reason, and the curtains stayed drawn for the entire journey.

If Quetta had been an attack on the senses, then Karachi was an all-of-body experience. The largest city in Pakistan, Karachi is a bustling hive of activity, coated in a dizzying haze of smog, sea spray and spices. The aromas of the bazaars infused with the blazing summer sun and humidity assaulted our highland senses like a slap in the face. But we had no time to take it all in as the bus turned off the main road and headed through an industrial area, eventually pulling up at an abandoned warehouse.

'You will stay here. Someone will come and get you when the time is right,' announced the driver, a moustachioed man with a big belly and chest hair bristling from the top his shirt.

'Stay where, exactly?' shouted a man from the back of the bus.

'Right here,' and the driver pointed out the window to where some crates and boxes lined one wall of the derelict building.

'And where will we be going today or tomorrow?' asked another man.

'I don't know. My job was just to bring you here. Now get your things and get off the bus.'

We did as we were told, collecting ourselves in a corner of the warehouse. As the bus rolled away and the warehouse door closed, we wondered if we would have to endure a night in this decrepit building. We began to feel suffocated in the crushing heat. With no contacts in Karachi and no money in our pockets, we just had to pray that the agents would honour their words.

As the sun climbed higher into the sky, we drifted into a hazy sleep, only to be woken by the sound of the gate opening, and then the warehouse door. A minivan rolled in with two men inside. The driver got out, followed by a man dressed in a smart suit.

'Listen up, everyone. We have plane tickets to Jakarta for you all,' said the man in the suit. 'You fly out tonight.'

We stood listening in eager silence.

'Now listen carefully. You must follow our instructions every step of the way. If we tell you to use a certain lane, use it. If we tell you to stand, sit, speak or shit, then you do *exactly* as you are told. Understood?'

The two men eyed us all like generals inspecting their troops.

'Family groups will go with us now. Another bus will come to pick up the singles.'

We stood ready to board the bus. Dad, keen to avoid another fuss over Mojtaba, hid his youngest son in a bag, carrying him like a bag of groceries. We climbed aboard the minivan with the other families. Dad had become close to some of the single men and hugged them goodbye.

'We will meet again. Inshallah.'

The minivan pulled out onto the main road, and before long we were on the highway to Jinnah International Airport. On arrival we were swept into a torrent of tuk-tuks and taxis.

Dad held my hand and I held Ali's as we followed the agent through the maze of people towards passport control. The queue wound through the reception area like a giant serpent coiled up in the sun. At the front of the line, immigration officials scrutinised every passport. We had clear instructions to go to one particular desk — the smugglers had paid off specific immigration officials to turn a blind eye to our forged visas. If we joined the wrong line, we were sunk.

We stood nervously in line. None of us had been in an airport before, and we were lost in a sea of television screens and alien sounds. We were inching forward in the queue and eventually saw the first family from our group pass through safely. Soon there was only one family ahead of us. I watched as the official scanned each passport carefully, taking extra care to pretend to scrutinise every detail as if he were actually doing his job. He flicked through the boarding passes and cross-checked them with the passports. After a few stern looks, the official stamped and returned the passports to the family.

Now it was our turn. As our family walked forward, a supervisor yelled at us from the other end of the hall: 'You! Small groups! The rest of you go to this lane!' He pointed to the immigration lane next to our designated one.

We froze. Dad held my hand and carried Mojtaba in the other. Mum, Sakhi, Ali and Shekufah were behind us.

'Come,' Dad whispered to us under his breath. 'You didn't hear that.'

'Smaller groups!' The supervisor marched towards us.

Dad dropped the stack of passports on the desk in front of us and gave the immigration officer a look I'd never seen before. It was utter desperation combined with boiling anger — all told through his eyes. The immigration officer flicked quickly through the passports and stamped Dad's and mine just before the supervisor arrived.

'It's all right, sir, I've got it,' he said to his boss. Before the supervisor could respond, his attention was mercifully diverted by a scuffle in another lane — some drama over the misspelling of a name.

The immigration officer stamped the rest of our passports and we hurried through the gate and out of sight of the supervisor.

Meanwhile, the agent had disappeared. He had done his job and we were through the toughest part. We hurtled through the giant terminal, gazing at screens in search of the boarding gate that matched the one printed on our boarding passes. We were too scared to ask for help in case we inadvertently tipped anyone off. Eventually we found it and settled to wait in nervous silence at the gate. Every minute went by as slowly as the spring snowmelt. We had spent our entire lives in the mountains, touching the roof of the world. Now we were about to board an aeroplane for the first time.

It was completely and utterly overwhelming.

We didn't sit near any of the other families in case we raised suspicion. It seemed everyone had made it through.

Eventually we boarded a shuttle bus to take us to the waiting aircraft. On the plane I was seated between Mum and Dad, with Mojtaba resting on Mum's lap. I felt as though I were in the belly of a giant bird that would take us far away from everything. Soon we were hurtling down the runway. I watched as the wheels lifted up, my insides churning. My only connection with land now was the shadow of the plane streaking across the buildings below. I gasped as cars and lorries became smaller and we climbed higher and higher.

It had been more than three months since we had left Sungjoy and I was tired to my bones. I dreamt about a place where I could run around with my friends, eat naan and go to school.

As we climbed into the heavens, the land below disappeared into a blanket of thick white cloud, erasing all the anxiety we had endured.

9.

THE

ISLAND

'BOAT PEOPLE' FIRST appeared on Australia's radar in the 1970s, with the arrival of Vietnamese refugees fleeing the war in their country. Although they were initially welcomed by the Australian government and a sympathetic society, the mood changed drastically throughout the 1980s. Changing demographics coupled with high unemployment provided a fertile breeding ground for racialised politics in local and federal government. The bipartisan support for the rejection of the country's White Australia policy was beginning to crumble. As such, the issues of race and multiculturalism trickled into mainstream politics, often appealing to voters' most tribal instincts. From 1984 onwards, Australia's asylum seeker policy swung from one of sympathy to suspicion. But it was not until 1992 that Canberra legislated the mandatory detention of asylum seekers who arrived in Australia by boat. Short detention for health and processing purposes is common practice around the world, but Australia alone has legislated to hold asylum seekers indefinitely. That policy continues today.

The practice proved popular with an Australian public that had grown unsympathetic to these 'illegals'. Bashing the boat people became a national sport. A 1998 poll showed that the average Australian overestimated the number of boat arrivals by a factor of 70. There seemed to be a prevailing perception of a 'genuine' refugee as one who would wait patiently at a camp for Australian immigration officials who would, in time, grant them the appropriate papers. These pesky boat arrivals were trying to jump the queue; they lacked the appropriate paperwork and were disorderly. Politicians campaigned to be tougher on these 'queue jumpers'.

Several misconceptions need clarification here.

First, there is no queue. Being approved as a refugee did not mean your file was assigned to the Australia or Canada or Norway out-tray. The total number of resettlement places in the world is oversubscribed a hundred times over, and the ultimate decision lies with the governments of those countries. The other 99 per cent of refugees must simply wait. And wait. It's not like a vaccine rollout, where you know that ultimately there will be enough doses for everyone and a little patience is all that is required.

Second, it is not illegal to claim asylum in a foreign country if you can prove that your home, and/or a transit country, is unsafe. Furthermore, the notion of 'a fair go' is central to New Zealand and Australian societies. How fair is it that refugees who are forced to flee death and misery at home, and have nowhere to go, are blocked from seeking a life of dignity and security? This right is enshrined in international law.

Indonesia is not a signatory to the 1951 Refugee Convention, and therefore not obliged to provide any assistance to refugees. However, over the years successive Indonesian governments have practised tolerance towards the existence of refugees in their territory, who nevertheless have no right to work, study or access social services.

Asylum seekers arriving in Indonesia hope that the UNHCR will approve them for resettlement, but this is where the limbo begins. Given the dismal resettlement statistics quoted above, their wait has only just begun.

In Indonesia the majority of asylum seekers (those who have not yet had their cases heard by the UNHCR) and refugees (those who have been interviewed and granted refugee status) live in detention centres run by the government. These are usually in abandoned buildings or overcrowded dormitories with no running water or electricity. The waiting period for resettlement approval can take years or even decades. I have two close family friends who, at the time of writing, have spent eight years in a detention centre in Jakarta, despite having been approved as refugees. They are caught in a web of bureaucracy and political indifference.

Where there is desperation, there is also illicit profit. People-smuggling operations capitalise on the misery of those ensnared in this hopelessness. When the Afghan civil war erupted, a trickle of refugees made it to Indonesia, accompanying others fleeing persecution in Iran, Somalia, Myanmar and elsewhere. Seeing a gap in the market, smugglers stepped in and offered places on boats to Australia — for a hefty price. Stripped of a past, facing a torturous present, desperate asylum seekers would place everything on the line for the sliver of a chance at an uncertain future.

WHEN WE STEPPED out on the tarmac in Jakarta, it was as if we had walked into an oven. The blistering heat and humidity reminded Mum of baking in the *tandoor*.

One of the other Afghan families had a contact in Indonesia, and through them we found accommodation in a rundown dormitory on the outskirts of Jakarta. It was like a student dormitory, with each boxy room hosting one family in a two-storey building with a communal bathroom and kitchen. It was an abandoned military accommodation block that had intermittent electricity and no running water except for one tap in the courtyard. The seven of us slept on the floor of a tiny room, surrounded by all our worldly possessions.

We had no idea how long we would be in Jakarta before a boat could be found for us. Days and weeks passed; five months after leaving Afghanistan we still did not know when our journey would end. Many of the families from our flight were in the same building and I became friends with the sons. Our little crew of half a dozen boys became a tight group. We were eager to explore our new home but dared not leave the building for fear of being caught by immigration officials. So our only entertainment venue was the courtyard, where we played football. One day one of the men came home carrying a box of tall glass bottles filled with some black liquid. Seeing us play in the courtyard, he handed us a bottle.

'Drink it. You'll like it. It's from America,' he said as he twisted the cap off.

Sweating from the choking humidity, I willingly took a swig. The strange black liquid immediately burned my throat and foam spurted out my nostrils. It was my first introduction to Coca-Cola and I swore never to drink the stuff again.

We lived on a diet of bananas, which I still detested after the incident in Quetta. Mi-Goreng instant noodles became a staple, and we would exchange packets to secure the coveted chicken flavour. Everyone was very low on funds by now. We all shared food; whoever had money would buy something and we would make it go around.

With no school, Dad's commitment to our education only increased. One Afghan man who had lived there for some time had a computer and printer. We had no idea how any of it worked, but most days he would update everyone on news from Afghanistan by reading out articles from BBC Farsi. Dad would ask him to print the page, which he would bring home for us to read and then write out.

As the days went by I could tell that Dad and the other men were getting more and more anxious. They had not heard from our agents in weeks. Some who had used a different agent had left weeks ago, but a few had returned after their boat was intercepted by the Indonesian coastguard. They had been held in immigration detention centres but a few had escaped. Back to square one.

A few of the asylum seekers had become veterans — some had tried multiple times to reach Australia only to be turned back. They were intercepted by the coastguard, or ran aground on a shallow reef, or ran out of fuel, or got lost, or had mechanical issues – or a combination of the above. Every time they would come back to square one and try again.

The plan seemed simple. A boat would ferry the asylum seekers out of Indonesian waters and into Australian territory. It didn't have to arrive at the mainland, just make it to the waters of any land under Australian sovereignty. For many, salvation lay on Christmas Island. This tiny outcrop in the Indian Ocean was 500 kilometres south of Jakarta and 2500 kilometres northwest of the Australian continent. Asylum seekers who made it to Christmas Island were entitled to have their asylum applications processed in Australia. You just had to make it to Christmas Island.

It was late August and a wave of homesickness washed over me. If we had been in Sungjoy we would have escaped the midsummer sun by diving into the creek. The apricots and pears would have just ripened, and we would be sleeping on the roof most nights. Instead, we were imprisoned within the walls of a rotting ex-military dormitory we could not leave. I hated it there.

I wished I could go back to Sungjoy and run through the valley once more.

I wanted my home.

10.
ALL
AT SEA

DAY 1, 23 AUGUST 2001

Seasickness. The moment the *Palapa* left the craggy shoreline, vomiting started. I began heaving, dry-retching and emptying my insides into a plastic bag. I was not alone. It spread throughout the boat like a plague, hitting women and children the hardest. Siblings shared plastic bags, one child's dinner mixed with another's lunch. Pretty quickly, the bags began filling up, and soon they covered the small amount of unoccupied floor. When the retching subsided, I tossed and turned in a bid to reclaim some of the night's sleep.

I was woken some hours later by the overpowering stench of vomit. Needing some fresh air, and to empty my insides from the other end, I followed Dad up to the deck. Each step brought us closer to sunlight, sea breeze and the distinct tang of the salty sea spray. Inside, it was hard to tell how fast we were moving, but from up here it was clear the boat was making good headway. Many others were up on deck – young men smoking, a few kids running around or simply looking over the edge, marvelling at the endless blue. Towards the stern was a small, boxy wheelhouse with a window where the captain stood. It reminded me of the Taliban checkpoint in Spin Boldak. A mess of tools, ropes, netting, fuel, water and emergency supplies littered the bow.

My desire to relieve myself disappeared when I saw the toilet. It was a phone booth with a hole in the floor through which the sea could be seen frothing beneath. Faeces were smeared liberally around the hole and across the exterior of the stern, thrown by timely wind gusts. I wondered if the barnacles were having a feast. This was the *Palapa's* one and only toilet. I walked back out and silently gripped Dad's hand as we rejoined the family.

WE WERE ON the level just below the top deck, and below us were two more levels. Most of the families were with us, while the lower levels were filled with those travelling alone. Protective mothers kept their children close for fear of losing them overboard. Any inch of space not occupied by bodies was taken up by belongings. Bags, luggage, bundles of clothing, food, water bottles, plastic bags littered every part of the boat.

A single staircase connected the levels and carried a constant flow of bodies going up and down as people took turns escaping the poisonous fumes and deafening whirr of the engine. Even during the day it was dark down below. It felt as if we were in a claustrophobic underground tunnel. Remarkably, though, people were in good spirits. We could taste freedom on the salt spray.

Anticipating a whole new life in a foreign country, we had packed just the bare necessities, as well as the odd small token of home. For Mum, it was the white scarf she had worn at her wedding. For Dad, it was the Quran that had sat above the door of our house in Sungjoy.

The boat's name, *Palapa*, is a Spanish word for a flimsy shelter roofed with palm leaves. Someone joked that it was actually the *Palapa 2*, as the first one had capsized. On that first day, as the *Palapa* cut through the waves, the mood remained buoyant. People were still throwing up, but there was a sense that every wave surmounted brought us a few metres closer to a new beginning.

Some of the men even became exuberant. Just look

at us! A boatload of land-loving mountaineers traversing one of the greatest oceans to begin a new life abroad. Who would ever have dreamt it?

That first day passed quickly as we familiarised ourselves with our new surroundings. The rushing water below, the sea spray above, the rancid smell around us — we had plenty to keep us busy. Morning turned into afternoon, which became evening. There was no sight of land ahead or behind. We were truly on our way.

BUT ANY EUPHORIA was short-lived. The trouble started with a loud bang, followed by a rhythmic hum and then silence. It was just after sunset and we had been motoring for around 15 hours. Now, like an overworked donkey, the engine appeared to have collapsed. Some of the men immediately got to work checking out the damage. It didn't take a genius to work out that the boat was overloaded and too heavy for the small engine. After some time it restarted and we began moving again, but a short while later the engine cut out a second time. This pattern continued for much of the night, and by sunrise the engine had died completely. The donkey had been whipped to its last breath.

The morning sun bathed the *Palapa* in a wave of

anxiety. With no way to get the engine going again, and without any radio equipment, we were hopelessly adrift. Dead in the water. Yesterday's excitement was replaced by fear and uncertainty, and discussions continued through the morning. Then a tanker was spotted in the distance. It was some distance away, and everyone on deck hurried to one side of the boat with such enthusiasm that the *Palapa* rolled violently. We waved and screamed to get the ship's attention, but it drifted by and disappeared over the horizon. It saved itself a lot of trouble.

We had to get moving somehow. Some paddles were found among the supplies, and bits of timber were stripped from the external framing. Seated neatly like navigators on a waka, various men took turns to paddle. The *Palapa* was now a rowboat. But these heroics did little to move the lumbering vessel. Further efforts were made to resuscitate the engine, but it was no use. It was ancient and had completely come off its mount, shearing the gears. No amount of number 8 wire would bring it back to life now.

As the sun set on the second day, we wondered at the cruelty of our situation. Just yesterday, we were on our way to a new life. Now we were drifting in the ocean, at the mercy of the waves. A helpless silence engulfed the boat.

Just as we were nodding off to sleep, the faint sound of a propeller plane broke the silence of the night. Those on the upper deck waved and shouted as they had done to the tanker. We couldn't see the plane in the black sky but the sound of the engine was unmistakable. The *Palapa* turned on its flimsy lamps, flashing them on and off. The plane seemed to be performing loops, the sound of its engine wheeling back and forth, but after a few minutes, it too disappeared.

God seemed to be toying with us.

DAY 3, SATURDAY 25 AUGUST

Another morning began. Some of the men had stayed up all night, on the lookout for any sign of rescue.

The ship's crew were all Indonesian; only the captain spoke some broken English. They appeared to have no idea how to fix the engine.

Morale was low. The ocean seemed angry, yesterday's blue replaced by a steely grey. The sky matched it. There was a darker patch of sea in the distance, as if God had spilled an ink pot on a grey page. People said a storm was brewing. Mum and Dad did their best to project calm but we could all tell they were uneasy. Dad was quieter than usual, and Mum looked forlorn in unguarded moments, the way she had looked when my sister had passed away.

We were all dehydrated and seasick, with Mojtaba the

most vulnerable. He had cried himself to sleep in Mum's arms the night before. Mojtaba had fallen ill within days of our arrival in Jakarta. Unable to visit a doctor for fear of being caught, Mum and Dad had put his sickness down to tropical heat and humidity and hoped for the best. But that morning he seemed particularly pale and lifeless.

We had been told it was only a two-day trip to Christmas Island, and everyone had packed just enough. With supplies now running low, tempers ran high.

Where there had been enough space for everyone on the first night, the boat now seemed to have shrunk. Families became territorial and defensive, sniping and snarling at one another. That's *my* water bottle. Don't move my bag. What are you looking at?

One of the men who had visited us that evening at the Gold Hajji's place had since become a close friend; I viewed him as an uncle. That morning he gave me a lemon sweet to stave off my hunger. As he turned his back, another man snatched the sweet from me. I don't know if he was playing a game to ward off boredom or if he really wanted the lolly but I let fly. Erupting like a volcano, I unleashed a torrent of abuse at the man, using every colourful word I had accumulated in my seven years. The man froze like a deer in the headlights as I volleyed insult after insult, even bringing his great-grandparents into disrepute.

'Abdul, control your boy!' the man said to Dad. 'I'll give the sweet back.'

'So don't fuck with him in the first place,' Dad sniped back with a cheeky grin on his face. Who knew his son had such an extensive vocabulary?

I sat down with my lolly to a wave of applause and laughter. I'd done my part to lift some spirits that morning.

Around mid-morning the distinct sound of propellors sliced once more through the grey sky. This time we could see the source of the sound — a small red and white turboprop flying high above us. It circled overhead like a vulture eyeing its prey. We cheered and waved at the plane, knowing this time that it had seen us. The plane continued to circle overhead as we awaited a sign that it acknowledged our distress. A flash of its lights. Dropping a rescue beacon. Anything. But the plane circled a few more times and then disappeared back the way it had come.

Had it seen us? Did the pilot know we were in trouble? Had they called for help?

As we pondered these questions the grey clouds that had been in the distance were now bearing down on the *Palapa*. We began to prepare for the coming storm, stowing our belongings and securing anything that could fly around. It was mostly the younger men doing this work. Those with children simply stayed put, out of the way.

Suddenly the now familiar sound of the propellors returned. The plane performed the same manoeuvre, circling us, this time slightly lower and for slightly longer. Where the morning's sighting had attracted those on the upper decks only, the afternoon's sighting drew everyone out of the hull. The *Palapa* lurched dangerously as hundreds of bodies crammed its deck. Those who had brought life-jackets waved them in the air. Dad held Mojtaba up in the air like Rafiki with Simba. Other parents did the same with their small children. Look! There are children on board! Help us!

Shouting, screaming, waving and praying, we watched as the plane circled one last time and disappeared into the horizon, as if it were fleeing the looming dark clouds.

Each sighting had raised our hopes, only to have them crash back down. As the sun set on our third day at sea, the heavens opened. Rain began pounding the *Palapa* from above, while the ocean pummelled it from below. The storm had arrived.

I REMEMBER WATCHING the *Palapa* falling to pieces before my eyes as each wave whacked its hull with a vengeance. Timbers cracked and split. Nails ripped away from boards. Water crashed over the deck and filtered down between the cracks, drenching us in hundreds of little salty waterfalls. The hatch had been closed, but a large hole had appeared as the decking fell apart.

The *Palapa* was taking on water. Men from the lowest level began bailing with buckets and plastic bags, forming a human chain up the ladder. Someone fashioned a pump out of engine parts. Others worked to seal the hole in the deck using ropes and a tarp, and some used more broken engine parts to hammer posts back in place. It would seem we were making good progress until another big wave crashed over us, undoing all our work. With the pump on full blast we seemed to be just keeping up, but after a few hours it too gave up the ghost.

The storm was relentless — the *Palapa* was like a bath toy at the mercy of an insolent child. With every toss of the boat we were helplessly thrown about, crushing one another in a sea of bodies. Luggage, clothing and plastic bags of vomit became random projectiles. In the darkness I couldn't make out if I was covered in shit, piss, water, vomit or all of the above.

I hung on to Dad, and he clung to his other children. He had wrapped a towel around a rafter and held it tight to anchor us, and undid his belt to make another handle for Mum. Seeing this, others followed suit.

The single men continued to bail water, undeterred by

setbacks in the form of fresh waves. The crew remained on the captain's bridge, no doubt knowing such efforts were futile. The *Palapa* fought bravely, but it was clear that it would not hold together much longer.

Then there was a stomach-turning plunge and a piece of the timber frame ripped clean off the side of the boat, leaving a gaping hole big enough to swallow a man. Someone quickly pulled a child aside just as a piece of luggage was sucked into the hole. A second later and that child would have disappeared into the nothingness. It was no more than two or three metres from where we were huddled.

Looking through the hole, all I saw was blackness. The only delineation between sky and sea was the water's surface, frothing like a rabid beast. Dad gripped me tight as others rushed to plug the hole with whatever they could find.

It was at this point that we began to give up hope. There had been four chances of rescue and none had happened. The likelihood of any craft offering assistance at night, in the pitch dark, was close to zero. People's screams became distant and hushed as they clung together, and a deathly silence took hold while the storm continued to rage.

The prayers began as urgent murmured exaltations, and soon everyone's silent prayers combined to become a single voice. The prayers grew louder and louder, each verse sung out in defiance of the waves. We entered a trance-like state, our prayers drowning the crash of the waves. Freezing seawater cut our flesh like razorblades.

It was *Du'a Kumayl* — the prayer of penance:

اللَّهُمَّ اغْفِرْ لِي كُلَّ ذَنْبٍ أَذْنَبْتُهُ وَكُلَّ خَطِيئَةٍ أَخْطَأْتُهَا

Oh Lord, forgive me every sin I have committed
and every mistake I have made.

IF THERE IS one thing I want you to take away from this book it is this. I want you to imagine being in a situation where the future — the very existence — of your family forces you to make an impossible choice. You have to choose whether to stay in the life you know and face misery upon misery, or leave and take a chance on the slightest sliver of unseen hope.

What would you do?

Having made our choice, our future was now totally out of our control. In leaving Sungjoy we had rolled the dice and got lucky. In crossing into Pakistan we had rolled the dice a second time. In setting our sights on Australia and climbing aboard the *Palapa* we had rolled the dice once more. Had our lucky streak come to an end? How could it not? How much luck could possibly be on our side?

Seeing Mum crying, I began to weep too. Tears rolled down her cheeks and onto Mojtaba's forehead. Even Dad was beginning to crumble. As the head of our household, Dad, like all the other fathers on board, was responsible for our being there. He had carried his family all this way, and now it was all falling apart. His dream of delivering us to safety was being shattered with every wave. He held himself solely responsible for our imminent deaths.

The cacophony of prayers was now dialling down to a few hoarse voices. On this tiny vessel surrounded by darkness in every direction, the prayers changed tack. We were no longer praying for salvation; we had accepted our fate. We prayed for death to free us from this suffering.

We had accepted that we would die that night.

يَا رَبِّ ارْحَمْ ضَعْفَ بَدَنِي وَرِقَّةَ جِلْدِي وَدِقَّةَ عَظْمِي

My Lord, have mercy upon the weakness of my body,
the thinness of my skin and the frailty of my bones.

Dad closed his eyes in silent prayer.

'Oh God, if we are to meet You on this darkest of nights, please grant us one last wish: that our bodies be washed ashore so that we may be buried on land.'

ABOVE LEFT One of the earliest photos of Dad. He would spend many years working away from his family. Mazar-e-Sharif, 1980s.

ABOVE RIGHT Mum and me at the age of one in the mid-90s in Sungjoy. The forces that would uproot our lives were beginning to emerge at this time.

BELOW Me with Mum and some of the other villagers at our homestead in Sungjoy, late 1990s.

OPPOSITE ABOVE Dad (green shirt) at a construction site in Iran.

OPPOSITE BELOW Ali, Hussein, Dad and me in the late 1990s. This was taken weeks before Hussein fled to Iran. You can see the anxiety on Dad's face.

LEFT First day of school in Pakistan, Sakhi was clearly not looking forward to it.

BELOW The *Palapa* alongside the *Tampa* on the day of our rescue. Captain Arne Rinnan saved our lives. © Wallenius Wilhelmsen/AAP

ABOVE The survivors of the *Palapa* on the deck of the *Tampa*. This is how we spent our days — sleeping in containers or on the deck under the burning tropical sun. © Wallenius Wilhelmsen/AAP

BELOW Being ferried from the *Tampa* (R) to the HMAS *Manoora* (L) as part of the 'Pacific Solution'. © Fairfax Media

ABOVE With Mum and Mojtaba in our driveway at Ballantyne Ave, 2003.

LEFT Mum with nine-month-old Mostafa during one of our regular picnics at the Botanic Gardens, Christchurch.

LEFT In front of our house at Ballantyne Ave on our first day of Riccarton Primary School, January 2002, with Jan, one of our family's volunteers.

BELOW Ali and I learnt about birthdays at school, and convinced Mum to throw a joint party to make up for all the years we'd missed.

ABOVE The Nazari clan a year into our lives in Christchurch, with only Hussein missing.

LEFT The third best speller in New Zealand on his first day of primary school, January 2002.

LEFT Being congratulated for my spelling achievements at the Hagley Homework Club in 2008 with Mum watching on proudly.

BELOW I've become lifelong friends with the other children of the *Tampa* — L-R: me, Mushi, Omid, Meysum and my brother Ali.

Fear was plastered on every face. Parents whispered their own prayers in Farsi between the Arabic passages.

The man next to us prayed for mercy for his children.

'Oh God, spare the children for they are innocent. Take me instead.'

Hot tears rolled down my frozen cheeks. I had no understanding of why we were in a boat out in the middle of an ocean far from home. I still did not fully grasp the forces that had propelled us to leave the mountains. I trusted and followed my father in those things. But at that moment I did understand one thing: we were about to die.

Even then, a boy of seven has no understanding of death. Will it be quick? Will there be suffering? Will I see my siblings again? What about my parents? Did I deserve to die? Why me? Why us? Why was God angry at us? The questions streamed through my mind as we were rocked by wave upon wave.

Soon enough, the praying stopped. Even the crying and puking and dry-retching stopped. All became deafeningly silent.

Everything blurred into the never-ending motion on a sea of black.

I do not know how long it was, and no one can now recall, but the darkness began to abate and there was a faint light. Soon daylight entered through the hole in the side of the boat. As the sun began to rise, the waves subsided to a gentle rocking and then a mild sway. The clouds dissipated and tears of joy washed away the darkness of the night.

God had heard the prayers of these poor Afghan mountain people above the thunder of the waves. And He had answered those prayers.

We were alive.

DAY 4, SUNDAY 26 AUGUST

Relief. Instant relief. The sort that fills your body with a soothing warmth. As if you've been drowning, clawing and gasping for air and you finally break the surface.

As the sun rose higher and the ocean calmed, relief bathed the boat. There was a renewed energy and the cleanup began. Men resumed bucketing. Parents wiped their children free of human waste. Bottles of clean water were passed around. Some men worked at plugging holes while others inspected the motor again. Perhaps divine intervention had also reached the broken engine.

On deck, a group of elders converged around the captain's bridge. The initial anger at being duped aboard this unseaworthy vessel was still palpable but nothing could be done about that now. What was done was done. The immediate concern was the condition of the boat, and rendering assistance to those who had been injured during the storm.

It was clear that the boat would not survive another night in its current state.

The limited food and water were being distributed among the women and children, more than a dozen of whom had been rendered unconscious. One boy had a broken arm, and two men had severe lacerations to their arms and legs. No one had died and, as far as we could tell, no one was missing. We had boarded as strangers but we were quickly becoming a team.

Most importantly, the conversation centred on why the plane had not acknowledged the boat — or come back with help. Surely the pilot had seen that the boat was in trouble. Or maybe not? Perhaps the pilot thought the children were being held up to see the plane, rather than for the pilot to see the children? We knew we were waving our arms and pleading for help, but perhaps that message was not being received?

There was a handful of English speakers on the *Palapa*. One of these was Shah Wali Atayee, a thin, wiry Hazara with jet-black cropped hair. The father of five had been a teacher in his village and had taught himself English as a young boy in Kabul. He would play a critical role as the story unfolded. As we looked out at the horizon, Atayee had an idea. Many years ago, he had read in an English novel that the letters SOS were used as the maritime distress signal. Save Our Souls.

People sprang to action. A few women wearing white headscarves took them off without a second thought and sent them to the top deck. Another had the idea to use engine oil to write the letters. The scarves were laid out on the deck in as much space as we could allow. Atayee painted the letters, using every drop of engine oil to ensure the message was unmistakable.

The words SOS and HELP glistened in the morning sun, surely visible from above.

There would be no mistake this time.

11.

THE GREAT

RED WALL

THE AUSTRALIAN COASTGUARD had most certainly seen us.

Canberra had classified the *Palapa* as a suspected illegal entry vessel, or SIEV. In the months and weeks before we set sail, as we discovered later, the number of SIEVs reaching Christmas Island had steadily increased. The day we boarded the *Palapa*, a SIEV carrying 359 people had landed on the island; a week earlier, another boat arrived with a further 345 asylum seekers. All of those on board had been taken to mainland Australia for processing.

Now the authorities kept close tabs on any SIEV detected. Bureaucrats inside the Department of Prime Minister and Cabinet and the Department of Immigration and Multicultural Affairs (DIMA) kept a watching brief on every such vessel, briefing their respective ministers as the situation unfolded. Information was gathered from a wide range of sources, including informants in Jakarta and naval intelligence. Coastwatch Australia, the civil agency that coordinated rescues, became aware of the *Palapa* on our second day and ordered a flyover.

That was the red and white turboprop we had seen. It had flown over from Christmas Island in the morning, reporting to the Australian Maritime Safety Authority (AMSA) in Canberra that the vessel 'appeared to be dead in the water', with about 80 people on board. The same pilot and plane returned in the afternoon, this time filming us. His second report updated the figure to '200-plus'. The second Coastwatch report noted that the vessel was in distress but that no call for rescue had been made. There was no official MAYDAY or SOS from the SIEV. Video from the Coastwatch plane shows the *Palapa* wallowing in a big swell. Had Coastwatch or AMSA called for assistance on the first or second flyover, then we might have been spared the night of the storm.

Not wanting to commit to any rescue, thereby assuming responsibility for those on board, Australian authorities had spent the evening trying to convince their Indonesian counterparts to intervene. As the storm battered the

Palapa that Saturday night, Canberra repeatedly called on Indonesia to act, and Indonesia continued to ignore them. We now know that the Australian Federal Police (AFP)'s people-smuggling unit, working on intelligence gathered from informants, had raised concerns with Coastwatch about the state of the vessel and the potential number of occupants. Coastwatch advised that the *Palapa* did not show signs of distress sufficient to constitute a call to rescue.

The next morning, Coastwatch was instructed to provide an update on the vessel, which had drifted some distance overnight. At 8 a.m. on Sunday the same pilot took off from Christmas Island in search of the *Palapa*.

'LOOK, IT'S BACK! It's the plane!'

Everyone turned to look. It was the same plane as yesterday. As it approached, we made the same frantic calls for help, waving energetically, and this time we had the painted sheet prominently displayed to help deliver the message. The plane circled for some time and headed off again. Anxiety swept through the boat as we contemplated another night on board. The storm had passed but there was no telling what the next night would bring.

Although we had no radio on board, was there not

some way the pilot could have signalled his intentions to rescue us? Could he not have dropped food or first aid or radio equipment? Or was this our fault? Was there some other rule about an SOS alert that we hadn't played by? We sat on deck in a mournful silence, time ticking by at a glacial pace.

The afternoon sun enhanced the foul stench of human waste, damp timber and seawater. Many children had developed skin lesions; I had angry, pus-filled sores on my thighs from sitting for days on damp timber. My skin cracked and bled whenever I walked. Ali had welts on the backs of his legs from sliding around during the storm. After three days at sea and having been drained of all bodily fluids, we were pale, hollow-eyed shells of our former selves.

Unbeknown to us at the time, our large SOS sign had shattered any illusions Coastwatch was under: clearly we were in distress after all. The script had now been flipped and a search-and-rescue operation was launched. Coastwatch relayed the information back to AMSA, which tried again to contact Indonesia.

Word had reached the office of Australian Prime Minister John Howard that the SIEV needed rescuing. DIMA called the Rescue Coordination Centre (RCC) at AMSA to ask whether the vessel or vessels that rescued the *Palapa* could tow it back to Indonesia. But the rules of maritime rescue dictate that the distressed vessel (assuming it could be towed) and its occupants must be delivered to the nearest port, which in our case was Christmas Island. Towing a rescued vessel further out to sea was unprecedented and contrary to established maritime norms.

It should have been clear-cut.

The call to rescue, which could have come the day before, finally went out at midday on Sunday 26 August 2001:

> *Distress Relay: A 35-metre Indonesian type vessel with 80-plus on board adrift . . .*

> *Vessel has SOS and HELP written on the roof. Vessels within 10 hours report best ETA and intentions to this station.*

I WAS DOZING, floating in and out of sleep, when a commotion woke me.

'Look, there's something on the horizon!' yelled someone from the captain's bridge.

Dad climbed up the hatch and put me on his shoulders.

'What do you see, my boy?'

'I don't know what it is. A black dot. I think it's moving.'

'Is it a ship? Is it coming towards us?'

A small black dot punctured the perfect line of the horizon. It was a fat upside-down triangle with a square on top. As it got closer, however, it began to take on an identifiable shape. A giant container ship was bearing down on us — in fact thundering rapidly closer, its prow parting the ocean like Moses, sending a tsunami either side of the red hull. The metallic hum of its engine grew louder and the hulking mass of metal resembled an otherworldly creature.

It was the *Tampa*.

CAPTAIN ARNE RINNAN had spent his entire career at sea. Working his way up from a deckhand, the 66-year-old now captained the *Tampa*, a 260-metre behemoth that was the property of Norway's Wilhelmsen Line shipping company. A grizzled, straightforward sailor with salt water in his veins, Rinnan, along with the Wilhelmsen Line, would become a central character in our story.

The *Tampa* had left Fremantle, Western Australia, a few days earlier, loaded mostly with heavy machinery. It was on its way to Singapore when Rinnan received the rescue call. Checking the coordinates of the *Palapa*, he instantly replied that he was four to six hours away and would chart a course to the rescue site immediately. With four decades at sea, Rinnan knew the laws of the sea like the back of his hand. It was the duty of any vessel to help another in distress.

With maritime law, Norwegian law and the reputation of a principled, century-old shipping company informing his decision, the captain confidently charted a course towards the *Palapa*.

EXCITEMENT GAVE WAY to panic. Had it seen us?

'Everybody move! Make noise! Get their attention! Make them see us!'

We jumped and shouted, waving the SOS sign frantically as the behemoth approached. There was general hysteria as we anticipated being crushed by the approaching red metal wall.

The *Tampa* veered off in a long swooping arc so that it was side on to our vessel. The square cubicles we had seen on board were large rectangular containers stacked like bricks. Towers of containers were stacked a dozen high.

The *Tampa* inched closer, revealing finer details. Faded

paint at the waterline. Red guard rails running the entire perimeter. We saw two men in orange jumpsuits standing near a folded ladder above us and uttered cheers and shouts of excitement. The *Tampa* was now so close that it blocked the entire horizon. The *Palapa* rolled in its wake.

There was a loud groan as if a giant had yawned, and the ship's propellers stopped. The gap between rotting timber and unforgiving metal closed further. Then there was a loud metallic clang from above and we all looked up to see the folded ladder reaching down like a giant metal hand. The bottom of the ladder hovered about two metres above the *Palapa*. Any closer and the swell would have smacked the ladder against the *Palapa*. The orange jumpsuits climbed down and one jumped onto the deck.

First officer Christian Maltau looked every bit the typical Scandinavian — not that I knew this at the time. Tall, blond and blue-eyed, he was the first white man I had ever seen. The other man stood on the platform at the bottom of the ladder.

'Can anyone speak English?' Maltau asked.

'Yes,' answered Atayee.

'Okay, good. You will all go up one by one. No bags. Just yourselves.'

Atayee relayed the message.

'One step at a time. Hand, foot. Hand, foot. Okay?'

Maltau continued, while the other man demonstrated.

'Don't look down. Only up!'

Nods of agreement and understanding all round.

'Okay, go! One by one!' Maltau ordered.

Those who were in good shape did not need any further encouragement. Maltau assisted in giving a leg up to any who could not reach the platform. The other sailor extended his hand, then moved aside while gesturing upwards. Rinnan, still in radio contact with Coastwatch, surveyed the rescue operation from the bridge.

A steady stream of survivors climbed the ladder, disappearing on a stairway to heaven. It was a long way up and we had been weakened by the last three days at sea. For many, the ladder may as well have been Mt Everest.

Tasked with packing mementoes from home for a life abroad, many had dug deep to bring small things they treasured. A Quran. A notebook. Photos. Now they were leaving them all behind. Nobody knew what would happen to the boat or its contents. Perhaps it would be lifted onto the *Tampa* or towed behind.

When it came to our turn, Sakhi led the way. He jumped forward, grabbing the little platform at the bottom of the ladder and hoisting himself up, no problem. Ali followed, with Dad lifting him like a prop at a lineout. Shekufah went up next as Ali and Sakhi waited at the platform to give Mum a hand. Those four continued to climb gingerly. Hand, foot, hand, foot, holding on for dear life.

Dad performed the same lineout move with me, with Mojtaba strapped to his chest with a towel. I reached out and grabbed onto the platform as if I were contesting the lineout with the ocean. From the platform of course I looked down, ignoring instructions to the contrary. The sliver of water between the two boats was calm, serene even. It seemed to be doing its best to help us. I looked up and grabbed the first rung of the ladder. Suddenly some superhuman strength kicked in and I was on autopilot, clambering confidently up the side of the vast ship. It was an out-of-body experience – I felt as if I were floating into the heavens, leaving behind the darkness of the past few days.

As I neared the top, my hands trembled.

'Don't stop, you're almost there!' I heard Dad's voice. He was only a few rungs below me.

I took one last look down at the *Palapa*. From above, it resembled a bloated barrel with one pointy end. It was surrounded by bits of debris and people's belongings. A stream of people followed behind Dad. From afar, we must have looked like a row of ants climbing up the leg of an elephant. I took a deep breath and powered on.

A sailor took my hand at the top and guided me past the railing. He pointed to another crew member, who was standing with a marker pen. He in turn held my left hand and wrote a number on my wrist. For the life of me I cannot remember what number it was, but everyone else I interviewed for this book fondly recalled theirs: 27. 54. 149. 221.

When Maltau had initially inspected the *Palapa* he had apparently radioed back that perhaps there were 80–100 people on board, so the actual number – 438 – must have been a shock.

People were sprawled across the deck as if we had crossed the finish line of an ultra-marathon. People hugged and kissed, exhausted and bewildered at the sudden change in fortunes. Some lay unconscious, with the healthy tending to them. Like drunks, many were leaning against containers, or lying down on what felt like solid ground. The crew dispensed biscuits and bottles of water.

I held Mum's hand as she knelt down, leaning against a container. She was near collapse and breathing heavily. This fit and healthy woman, who had spent every day fetching water, tending to animals, chopping wood, cooking, cleaning and caring for her many children, was near collapse. Having always had two feet on solid ground, it was during the climb that Mum discovered she had a fear of heights. It was a miracle she made it.

We were spread around an area that resembled a town square. Containers were stacked high above us on two sides, with a view of the ocean visible on the third side, and the captain's bridge at the other end. The rectangular open deck space would become our bedroom, living room, bathroom, prayer hall and town square all in one.

Two hours after the *Tampa* arrived, the last person climbed off the *Palapa*. Mum was one of only 26 females, two of whom were pregnant. Mojtaba was the youngest of 43 children. Dad was one of 369 men. All up, the *Palapa* was carrying 438 souls. Not including the captain and crew, there were 433 asylum seekers. Except for a handful of Pakistanis and Iranians, we were all Hazara Afghans.

Maltau inspected our boat and deemed it was unsalvageable. The structure was so compromised that it would likely disintegrate in the *Tampa*'s wake. And, as if to prove him right, minutes after the ladder was raised the *Palapa* succumbed to the ocean, swallowed in a daze of froth and bubbles. I watched the boat break up in a violent seizure and, within minutes, vanish beneath the surface of the Indian Ocean. Some debris floating against the side of the *Tampa* was the only evidence of its existence.

The *Palapa* had taken everything. We had nothing but the clothes on our backs.

But we were alive. God had granted us another day and for that we were eternally thankful. I cannot find the words to describe the feeling that washed over me at that moment. Twelve hours earlier we had been huddled together awaiting the cold embrace of death. Now, our would-be coffin was in a watery grave and we were floating in the sky.

It was like a dream.

12.
STAND-OFF

WITH THE *PALAPA* now out of sight, the *Tampa* began moving.

'Where are you taking us?' Atayee asked Maltau.

'We are headed for Singapore. Can you go with us to Singapore?' Maltau replied in the straightforward fashion we would come to know.

'No – please take us to Christmas Island. We must go to Christmas Island.'

Other men began gathering around the two.

'That is a decision for the captain to make,' said Maltau. 'I will have to talk to him.' He radioed Rinnan, who invited a small delegation to his bridge.

Those closest to Maltau formed a huddle. A decision

was made to send five English speakers. The all-male delegation had clear instructions from the rest of the group – to show gratitude and respect to the captain for rescuing us, and to find out where he was taking us.

While the rescue operation was taking place, we now discovered, Rinnan had already planned to set course for Christmas Island. As noted, maritime rules dictated that rescued survivors were to be disembarked at the nearest port. Christmas Island was only four hours away, and the obvious choice. If the drop-off went smoothly, Rinnan reckoned the *Tampa* could be back on course to Singapore by nightfall, and this rescue would add to the exciting tales of his long career at sea.

However, he had then received a call from the Indonesian search-and-rescue authority. Canberra had been pestering Indonesia for the past 24 hours to take the survivors and they had finally relented. Rinnan was instructed to disembark the survivors at Merak, a port on the island of Java, some twelve hours away. Rinnan was confused by this but reset his course once again, this time for Merak. Canberra must have breathed a sigh of relief. Their efforts over the past 48 hours had paid off: no one from the *Palapa* would be setting foot on Australian soil.

Minutes later, our delegation arrived with Maltau on the bridge of the *Tampa*.

'Thank you for saving our lives. We almost died. You saved us from death,' said a member of the delegation.

'We are from Afghanistan – and other countries. We have left behind everything we own. The situation is not good in Afghanistan and if we go back we will be killed.'

Rinnan explained that he had initially intended to head to Christmas Island but was ordered to chart course for Indonesia.

'Please do not take us back to Indonesia. There is nothing for us there. Please take us to Christmas Island.'

A tense silence followed. Rinnan, a master of the seas, was not one to crack under pressure, but the rescuees' desperation was written all over their faces. He sympathised with their plight. He had previously been involved in the rescue of Vietnamese and Cambodian boat people fleeing the atrocities of the 1980s.

In broken English, other members of the delegation spoke up to reinforce their distress, forgetting the instruction to show respect.

'We will jump off this boat if you do not take us to Christmas Island.'

In the middle of this exchange the Australian Maritime Safety Authority's RCC, which was being harassed by officials in Canberra for a minute-by-minute update, radioed the bridge for a status report.

Rinnan wanted to know if he could rechart for Christmas Island, given the stand-off. The RCC clearly favoured the Indonesian option, but the caller replied that it was ultimately Rinnan's decision, affirming another long-established maritime rule: that a ship's captain has overall command of his vessel at sea.

Maltau had briefed him about the numbers on board, and also the medical situation, so Rinnan knew the *Tampa* was now unseaworthy. There were nowhere near enough life-jackets or supplies for an extra 400 people. Christmas Island was the only rational option. 'Alright. We will go to Christmas Island.' The captain assured the delegation they would see the lights of the island before midnight. Then he radioed his intentions to Coastwatch and proceeded to turn the massive ship around once more.

Delegation members bounded down the stairs to deliver the news. There was instant jubilation. There were tears of joy and laughter. We would soon be on dry land! I jumped up and down with my siblings, suddenly finding renewed energy. Dad put me up on his shoulders and we walked alongside a wall of containers towards the ship's stern. We watched the massive wake forming behind the *Tampa* as the ship manoeuvred in a slow arc toward Christmas Island.

Rinnan had the crew open five empty containers.

Three of these would form our makeshift accommodation, and the other two were rigged with plastic buckets to make latrines. Hot soup was delivered from the kitchen in polystyrene bowls. Some crew members tended to those needing medical assistance. Of greatest concern were about a dozen women and a couple of young boys who had collapsed. The *Tampa* crew were incredibly accommodating.

As the sun began to set, someone suggested a group prayer. Those who could, stood shoulder to shoulder facing the sun. From the bridge, Rinnan snapped a photo of this motley band of survivors bowing in unison. I could not follow the Arabic of the prayer but, standing alongside my father, I performed the motions anyway. Despite my not understanding a word, it was the most spiritual experience of my life. It was a soothing communion, in stark contrast to the chaotic cacophony of prayer on the *Palapa* the night before.

Morning and evening prayers would become the two bookends of every day on board the *Tampa*.

IN TIME, CANBERRA would paint Rinnan's sudden departure towards Christmas Island as a potential hijacking. In their minds, a rescue operation had given way to a hostage situation. This played perfectly to their narrative of boat people as dangerous criminals. In interviews after the *Tampa* affair, Rinnan recalled the tension of that initial discussion on the bridge, where the anxiety level was undoubtedly elevated by the lack of English among the rescuees.

'Some of the men were behaving in a very excited manner,' Rinnan said, 'but I was not blackmailed.' He said he understood what the men were getting at, and never felt intimidated. At no point did he feel he was losing mastery of his vessel.

Meanwhile, as the *Tampa* steamed towards Christmas Island, Canberra was furious at Rinnan. A senior officer from DIMA directed the captain to turn his ship around. Australia was closed. He threatened to prosecute the *Tampa* captain under the Migration Act, making him liable for fines of up to $110,000 and a jail term. To the Australian government, Rinnan was no longer the captain of a vessel that had performed one of the most dramatic rescues in modern maritime history, saving hundreds of lives. He was a criminal.

Rinnan was bewildered and sensed political forces at play. Not wanting to wade into any political fray, he complied and turned away from Christmas Island for a second time. Many on board sensed the change of direction, or were alerted by the change in wind and stars. Murmurings turned to restlessness as some sensed that salvation was being taken away by stealth.

The delegation protested to Maltau as a few men began to get agitated. About six women were still unconscious, and some of the emaciated young children were not able to take any food or water. We urgently needed to get to land.

Maltau relayed the message to Rinnan. Sensing the potential for disorder, Rinnan had another change of heart and turned the ship towards Christmas Island for a third and final time. What had started as a rescue operation was becoming something he did not recognise. He was a proud ship's captain with decades of experience working with one of the most storied shipping lines in the world. The threatening messages from Australia went against all the maritime rules he had upheld all his life.

Rinnan faxed the RCC to say he was headed to Christmas Island and would anchor offshore until daybreak.

It was approaching midnight when the lights of Christmas Island appeared on the horizon. The night was clear and we could make out the shape of the island against the darkness. Many who had been asleep were woken by the excitement. Maltau told us we could not disembark until we had been given approval, and this would not be until after daybreak.

With the lights of the island in view I lay down next to Dad. After all we had been through, I didn't mind the cold floor of the men's container. It was only going to be one more night.

DAY 5, MONDAY 27 AUGUST

I needed to use the bathroom several times throughout the night. Every time, the buckets were a little more full. After the dehydration and seasickness we had suffered, the little food and water we had taken sparked a wave of diarrhoea, and a foul stench emanated from the latrines.

While many slept, an equal number stayed awake, eyes firmly set on the island. Rescue was so close, they were not going to let it slip away again. They could not sleep.

A handful of people were hysterical. The trauma of the last three days had finally caught up to them and they wailed uncontrollably as if reliving that hellish night on the *Palapa*. Maltau and the rest of the crew did their best to help, offering food, water, blankets, a small amount of privacy. They also brought out large buckets of clean water so we could wash our hands and faces. Hospitality is a core tenet of Afghan culture and we were grateful to our hosts.

For breakfast the next morning the cook prepared hard-boiled eggs and bread. They were not resourced for such a large-scale rescue, and over the coming days we would clean out their entire food supply. It reminded me of the bread and onion meal that had been a staple in Sungjoy and I wolfed it down. As we sat on the floor enjoying our first proper meal in days, Maltau relayed the message that the *Tampa* was still awaiting authorisation to enter the harbour.

What we didn't know was that Rinnan was engaged in yet another stand-off with Australia. Still incensed that Rinnan had disobeyed their orders, Canberra announced that the *Tampa* would not be permitted to land the survivors at Christmas Island or any other Australian territory. Even though the *Tampa* had rescued asylum seekers and was now within swimming distance of an Australian port, Rinnan would have to look elsewhere.

Rinnan was incredulous that Canberra would take such measures against a commercial vessel that had responded to an Australian rescue call. He radioed back that in light of the medical situation on board, the best course of action would be to land at Flying Fish Cove, the port at Christmas Island. About a dozen women were in dire need of medical attention, there were not enough IV drips to go around, and although some of the crew had basic first aid skills, there was no doctor on board. The two pregnant women also needed medical assessment.

By noon, as the stand-off with Canberra continued, the sun began to turn the deck into a *tandoor*. With no cover and no shoes, we began to bake under the sweltering heat, which worsened the condition of many survivors.

While most of the men were in better health, we children carried the scars of the journey most acutely. They say the concept of time disappears when you are on the water. We were proof of that — we had aged far beyond our years in the past three days. The constant vomiting and diarrhoea had sucked the life out of our bodies, like a tube of toothpaste squeezed to the very end. Our skin lesions were now angry sores and boils that cracked and bled in the hot sun. Hollow-eyed and lethargic, with pale faces and bleeding skin, we could have been cast as extras in a zombie thriller.

One boy had developed a bad fungal infection on his scalp. As a precaution, the crew had all of the children's heads shaved to prevent an outbreak of lice. To help with our various skin conditions, the sailors brought out a large metal tub and filled it with warm water. Parents were asked to scrub their children with a waxy green medicinal solution. I remember the bath well; Mum vigorously scraped my encrusted skin, eager to see me return to good health.

Still the *Tampa* remained at anchor as the stand-off continued for the rest of the day.

Some men went on a hunger strike. It was unbearable to be within sight of land and yet not be allowed any further. They let it be known they would refuse to eat or drink anything until they could land on the island. Rinnan relayed this message but Canberra held firm. Australia remained closed.

Dinner for the rest of us consisted of chocolate bars and milk. It was the first time I had eaten chocolate and I still remember the taste of those bars.

With no further word from Canberra we settled in for another night, this time sleeping on flattened cardboard boxes that the crew had found. As the lights on Christmas Island came on, we could make out several buildings.

We could almost reach out and touch them.

13.

A GAME
OF POLITICS

LIFE MAY HAVE been on hold for us, but in Canberra things were moving at lightning speed.

Officials within the Department of Prime Minister and Cabinet and DIMA gathered in the prime minister's office for crisis talks. They knew that preventing the *Tampa* from disembarking at Flying Fish Cove went against their legal and moral obligations. It was almost unprecedented to prevent rescued survivors from landing ashore, but they were keen to make a strong response to these boat people. And fast — the *Tampa* was a breaking story and Canberra needed to get a firm grip on how it played out. After all, it was election year.

Prime Minister John Howard was seeking a third

term in office, but if early polling was any indication, he would be out of office come November. The opposition Labor Party was comfortably ahead, riding a wave of voter dissatisfaction with the government's economic reform programme. Having walked the halls of the Australian parliament for nearly three decades, Howard had developed a potent talent for communication that was precise and yet vague at the same time. He would use this skill to full effect in the course of the *Tampa* affair, and become a central character in the story.

Also central is the role of the media. Coverage of Australia's 2001 election saw the rise of American-style media tactics of focusing on the person, rather than the policies. This would play in Howard's favour as he exploited the *Tampa* affair to position himself favourably in the eyes of the Australian public.

Although the polls showed that voters were primarily concerned with the economy and taxes, the issue of boat people was starting to gain some traction. Asylum seekers fleeing the conflicts in Iraq and Afghanistan had filled the detention centres on the Australian mainland beyond capacity. A system that was designed to hold a few hundred people was at breaking point, with the number of people arriving increasing from a few hundred per year in the mid-1990s to more than 3000 by 1999. Officials from DIMA had been sent to Jakarta to stem the arrival of boats by busting the smuggling syndicates, but the boats kept coming.

Asylum seekers were housed in decrepit living conditions administered by an indifferent bureaucracy. Having fled the cruelty and barbarism of Saddam Hussein and the Taliban, many who reached Australia now found themselves under an apparently endless prison sentence in a remote desert camp. Riots and protests were escalating. Hunger strikes were a common form of protest, with some inmates literally stitching their lips shut. There were many suicide attempts, with only the most extreme cases receiving medical or psychiatric help.

Demonstrations at the Woomera detention centre in the South Australian desert led to a mass breakout in June 2000. The facility, which was built to house 400, was home to some 1500 asylum seekers at the time. Following the recent legislative changes providing for indefinite detention (from the previous limit of nine months), many of the asylum seekers had been detained for nearly three years. A review later found that more than 80 per cent of them had legitimate grounds for asylum.

International media was now firmly focused on the demonstrations and protests, with camera crews training their lenses on the cramped facilities, tearful children and unarmed inmates facing off against security personnel wielding tear gas and water cannons. Australia's reputation was in tatters, and it seemed the government, already trailing in the polls, had lost control. Something had to be done.

Howard, sensing an opportunity, pounced on the *Tampa*. Here was a chance to put an end to the asylum seeker issue, once and for all.

Officials were tasked with working out how to get the *Tampa* out of Australian waters, out of sight of the media, and out of the minds of Australian voters. Government lawyers, immigration and customs officers and defence force personnel were told the *Tampa* was not Australia's problem and they were to make it disappear. Canberra had decided to deny the survivors their legal right to asylum and that was that. The Department of Foreign Affairs and Trade was to contact Norway and Indonesia and tell them to sort this one between themselves.

DAY 6, TUESDAY 28 AUGUST

With my skin starting to heal, and the cardboard offering some respite, I managed to sleep better that night. It was incredible how much difference a thin piece of cardboard made. Diarrhoea, nausea and dehydration still afflicted many of the children, and the men were quietly continuing their hunger strike. For the dozen or so who were still unconscious the situation had worsened. The ship's supply of IV fluid had been depleted. Rinnan was pleading to Canberra for medical assistance, but his calls went unanswered.

The third day on the *Tampa*, like the others, began with a prayer. With another hot day looming, Maltau and the crew, along with some of the men, rigged up a sunshade using large tarpaulins fastened to the second level of containers, providing a welcome reprieve. We huddled underneath, some nursing injuries and the men drawing strength to continue their protest in the sweltering heat.

It was in the welcome shade that I made friends with the other children. Along with my siblings there was Zaki, Mehdi, Omid, Mushi, Hadi, Zarif and two Alis. We were all little Hazara kids, plucked from Ghazni, Kabul, Mazar-e-Sharif and Bamiyan. We passed the day in the containers next to the latrines, laughing at one another's shaved heads, comparing scars and picking scabs.

Unbeknown to us, the *Tampa* affair had dominated news coverage for the past 48 hours. Wilhelmsen, the Norwegian shipping line that owned the vessel, decided to use the media to explain their situation. They asked the captain to provide the public with an insight into life on board the *Tampa*.

Speaking via radio, Rinnan spoke of the hunger strike, and pleaded for medical assistance for individuals in dire need. He confirmed that he was not being held hostage, as some columnists had asserted. Above all, he confirmed his desire for a quick and orderly resolution to the saga, and urged against any sort of military intervention.

The grainy photo of us standing in orderly prayer was faxed to media outlets, providing the outside world with their first glimpse of our group. In fact it would be the only image the world would see of the people at the centre of the brewing storm. Throughout the entire saga, Australian viewers would see no human face for the story. To readers and viewers, we were a group of 433 nameless and faceless foreigners.

DAY 7, WEDNESDAY 29 AUGUST

We had been at sea for a full week. We were so near and yet so far from salvation, and some of the solo teenagers were showing signs of severe mental distress. As the eldest sons, they carried the weight of their families' aspirations, and for many it was the first time they had ventured further than their villages. There were frequent threats of jumping overboard — a few who tried were pulled back from the brink. Maltau ran around with fluids, blankets and whatever else he could find to nurse the two pregnant women, but of course there was no way of knowing the condition of the babies.

Rinnan had had enough. Sensing the deterioration all around him, on the morning of the fourth day aboard the *Tampa* he issued a MAYDAY, demanding immediate medical assistance or permission to enter Flying Fish Cove. When the news reached us, we were cautiously optimistic. Rinnan had our best interests at heart. Surely now, Canberra would end the stalemate. No one was celebrating yet, however. After so many false starts, no one would believe it until they were actually on dry land.

But Rinnan's call was met with the most severe threat so far. Canberra dismissed his assessment of the conditions aboard his own vessel, and threatened that all options were on the table if he edged the ship any closer to the island.

Perhaps he was sick of having his judgement questioned and his seniority disrespected. Maybe he had finally had enough of Canberra's disregard for maritime law, or perhaps he feared for the safety of everyone on board, not least his crew. He knew that once he reached port, everyone who saw the state of the rescuees would wonder why he had not docked sooner.

Whatever his thinking, Rinnan turned on the engines and headed into Flying Fish Cove.

Christmas Island was now swarming with media, but Canberra had closed off the port and many other parts of the island to journalists and others. They declared *Tampa* a no-go zone, barring anyone from nearing the ship, including media and any local lawyers or doctors. Media coverage of the event was thus carefully managed; the only image shown was a stock photo of a red container ship in a blue sea.

As the *Tampa* came closer in we saw the sheer cliffs that edged the island, and the small inlet that led to the main town. We saw an observation tower and a runway, and larger buildings dotted about sporadically. People in colourful shirts waved at us from shore.

We later heard that the locals were all wondering why Australia was blocking the *Tampa*'s arrival, given how many other boats had arrived before and had been duly processed without fuss. Christmas Island community leaders had even signed a letter urging Canberra to grant Rinnan permission to make landfall.

But Canberra remained resolute.

Over the past 48 hours Canberra had apparently made a number of promises to Rinnan, including a helicopter full of supplies and a crew of trained medical personnel. None of the promises eventuated. Canberra was in fact otherwise engaged in convening a welcome party of a different kind.

As the *Tampa* neared the port, Rinnan was persuaded to go no further, as a boat carrying doctors and medical supplies would meet the ship in the harbour. Two rigid-hulled inflatable boats (RIBs) were duly seen hurtling out from shore — but what no one on board the *Tampa* knew was that they were actually carrying dozens of Australian Special Air Service (SAS) personnel. It was a trap. The RIBs, which were not flying a flag, reached the *Tampa* within minutes.

Maltau was waiting to greet the doctors when Rinnan radioed him urgently to pull up the ladders. Rinnan had vehemently opposed soldiers aboard his vessel at every turn, but it was too late. Before Maltau could register the command, the soldiers were climbing aboard.

They immediately surrounded our 'town square'. They were completely in black — black helmets, black visors, black combat boots and black fatigues. They were armed with guns that put the Taliban's AK-47s to shame. Some people screamed and shouted in horror. In Afghanistan a masked man with a gun usually meant death — or worse.

The first two RIBs were followed by several others, each one disgorging up to a dozen soldiers. In total, we had been welcomed by a party of 40–50 soldiers.

We were told we were now under the command of a Major Khan. With a name like that, we wondered if he could speak Farsi. In Afghanistan 'Khan' is a title given to rulers, as in Genghis Khan, and it was clear that The Major was indeed the new ruler on the *Tampa*. But he did not address us or explain what was happening. Instead, he directed his men to supervise us while Maltau took him to meet Rinnan on the bridge.

The horror of seeing those black-clad soldiers remains with me today – and with many others who were there. They did not speak, and we couldn't make out what they thought about us. Were we their prisoners? Would they kill us if we continued the hunger strike? What would happen to the rest of us if someone jumped overboard? Is this how Australia welcomed asylum seekers? Frozen in fear, no one uttered a word.

TEN YEARS LATER, Peter Tinley, the second in command of the SAS operation on that fateful day, would provide his perspective. He told media that despite being briefed and prepared for a potentially hostile and dangerous environment, the SAS found '400-plus ordinary refugees, very hungry, some who needed some medical attention, very scared and uncertain about what was happening, [and] a particularly concerned sea captain who just wanted to offload his human cargo and discharge his duty according to international law'. For all the drama of the moment, Canberra had essentially deployed the most highly trained troops in Australia to seize an unarmed, anchored vessel — a task that could easily have been performed by the local harbourmaster.

On the bridge, The Major reassured Rinnan that despite dozens of heavily armed soldiers commandeering the ship, Rinnan supposedly remained the master of the vessel. None of us were on the bridge during the exchange, but I imagine it was similar to the famous 'I am the captain now' scene from the 2013 film *Captain Philips*. The pirates were in fact firmly in charge but they needed the captain to sail the vessel. The Major directed Rinnan to steer the ship back to open ocean and out of Australia's territorial waters. Only then, he said, would medical assistance be given.

Rinnan knew it would be against Australian and Norwegian maritime law for him to head out to the open ocean when the *Tampa* was within sight of a port. Carrying more than 400 asylum seekers in various states of ill-health away from an available port and out to sea without life-jackets or life-rafts would break all the rules. The *Tampa* was currently unseaworthy by all legal definitions.

Rinnan refused to comply and another stalemate was reached. Wilhelmsen HQ, listening via an open line in the bridge, supported their captain's decision. There was no way of forcing Rinnan to leave the ship without commandeering the vessel, which would have constituted an act of piracy by Australia's most elite soldiers.

Sometime later, a small boat arrived carrying the doctors and medical supplies that Australia had promised two days earlier. I remember seeing the doctor walking along the rows of people with a clipboard in hand, while two soldiers walked alongside. Each checkup involved a quick glance up and down the rows of people. More time was given to those who needed it but the medical assessment was over in less than half an hour. The doctor reported that the health of those aboard was 'reasonable', and the SAS reported this to Canberra.

Back in Australia, while commending the bravery of the SAS in confronting a hostile environment, John Howard used this doctor's report to call into question Rinnan's assessment of conditions aboard, and the alleged need for Australia to allow the people to disembark. Splicing his comments between footage of the SAS boarding party, Howard, with the help of Immigration Minister Philip Ruddock, was further curating the image of a 'tough on immigration' strongman that would ultimately win him the election.

But Howard had bigger plans. That evening he introduced before parliament one of the most contentious pieces of legislation in modern Australian history. The Border Protection Bill or, to give it its official name, *The Bill for an Act to provide for the removal of ships from the territorial sea of Australia, and for related purposes*, gave sweeping powers to the government to refuse entry to anyone seeking asylum in Australia. It was designed explicitly to allow the government to block us from seeking asylum. The Act would be made retrospective to 9 a.m. that day, 30 minutes before the *Tampa* entered Flying Fish Cove.

MEANWHILE, ABOARD THE *Tampa*, everything was suspended. With a total media blackout we may as well have been floating in outer space. Nothing and no one was to leave the *Tampa* without SAS approval. No one could board the *Tampa* without approval. The Australian government was determined to deny the voting public any glimpse of us, any details of our stories or the reality of life on board. We were not fellow human beings desperately fleeing death and torture; we were pawns in a political game. We were an issue of national security.

The strategy was carried out with surgical precision while we were held at gunpoint.

14.

AUSTRALIA
IS CLOSED

DAY 8, THURSDAY 30 AUGUST

The second week at sea, our fourth day aboard the *Tampa*, began as usual with a prayer, except this time we had dozens of SAS members watching. We had not seen Maltau or the rest of the crew since the SAS had come aboard. With camcorders in hand, the soldiers were filming everything. From our prayers, to using the latrines, to the sad state of those on hunger strike.

That morning we were not served plates of food as usual. Instead, two soldiers placed a large bucket of berry jam in the middle of the deck and walked away. A couple of hungry young men, lured by the sweet treat, lunged at it. Then, realising the SAS were filming their desperation, the teens were outraged and made their feelings known. The soldiers reacted swiftly, pinning one of them down on the ground, then leading him away in handcuffs. The boy's brother rushed to his defence and he, too, was taken to the ground, handcuffed and marched out of sight.

In Afghanistan, being arrested and led away by men with guns meant at the very least a severe beating. A group of men started calling for the boys to be released. Sensing a growing protest, the soldiers formed a perimeter around the group, fire hoses at their hips like machine guns. Then The Major appeared and the tension settled when he ordered that the two young men be released.

Had the soldiers really set a trap and filmed our desperation as some kind of sick joke? In recent years, and especially during election cycles, the language and imagery around refugees and asylum seekers has been hyped up by right-wing politicians to exacerbate divisions. Suspected illegal entry vessel. Unauthorised boat arrivals. Queue-jumpers. Illegal aliens. National security threat. The language is designed to divide, dehumanise and denigrate. We had no doubt, in retrospect, that the footage of us was another tool to further their framing of us as dangerous and uncivilised. While the footage from the *Tampa* has not been made public, we would see this play out to full effect during the 'children overboard' scandal, a political fabrication to portray asylum seekers as savage and heart-less creatures who would deliberately throw their own children into the ocean.

With the crew no longer on deck, and with our hesitation to move about more than necessary in the presence of the soldiers for fear of being punished for doing so, the town square soon became filthy. The latrines stank, and the overflowing buckets were replaced with plastic bags. No one wished to clean the latrines and risk being punished for moving about without reason. Plastic plates and food scraps littered the deck as rubbish collection stopped. It was like a town falling into disrepair; the square was becoming uninhabitable.

WITH NO CONNECTION to the outside world, we had no idea that the *Tampa* affair had become a global story. It garnered daily headlines and was now pulling other countries into its orbit. The Norwegian Ministry of Foreign Affairs, incensed that Australia had escalated a maritime rescue into a military operation, wondered why, after all, such a wealthy democracy was refusing to accept the asylum seekers.

Indonesia, observing that the *Tampa* was firmly in Australian territory, bluntly refused to become involved.

Canberra even sought help from East Timor, which had just emerged from a bloody civil war as the world's newest country and was still under the auspices of the United Nations. Kofi Annan, the secretary general of the United Nations, politely declined. Australia, undeterred, initiated high-level talks with the United States, New Zealand, Papua New Guinea and Nauru.

A twofold plan was brewing in John Howard's office. First, stop any boats heading towards Australia. Second, ensure that the few that made it were processed offshore. This had the twin benefits of taking the load off the bloated detention centres in mainland Australia, and locating any new asylum seekers far away from media scrutiny.

On the afternoon of 3 September 2001 Howard unveiled part one of his masterplan. Under 'Operation Relex', Canberra would direct the Australian Defence Force (ADF) to form a blockade of Christmas Island and other Australian outposts to turn back boats. It was a show of force to discourage asylum seekers, while assuring Australian voters the problem was being resolved. Many in the ADF were apparently taken aback at this announcement. This would be an immensely expensive exercise, and even with every naval asset on full alert they could not provide complete coverage.

Howard did not go public with his plan for offshore

processing as the details had not been finalised, but his officials were hard at work. They just needed to find some rocks in the Pacific that would agree (for a price) to host their offshore processing centres. Nauru, a destitute island 7000 kilometres away, seemed perfect. The smallest republic in the world, most of its 12,000 inhabitants survive on fishing and foreign aid. Since the island's phosphate reserves had been hollowed out, chiefly by British and Australian companies, its economy was on life support. Canberra bargained with Nauru, offering to clear the island government's fuel bills for their generator-run desalination plants.

Around the same time, New Zealand answered Canberra's call. In Wellington, Prime Minister Helen Clark had been watching the *Tampa* saga with growing interest. When Canberra asked for assistance, Clark was told by her officials that the country's only refugee resettlement centre, at Mangere in Auckland, could accommodate only 150 refugees at a time, and a group of 80 were scheduled to arrive in a few weeks. Clark tasked Lianne Dalziel, her immigration minister, with finding a solution.

OF COURSE WE knew none of this. Our news from the outside world was restricted to short briefings from

The Major. He would come down from the bridge each afternoon to update us on the situation. One day The Major told us emphatically there was no chance we would ever set foot on Christmas Island. The Australian government was exploring other options for us, but he could not say more.

Upon hearing this, several people decided to write letters formally requesting asylum. Many handwritten letters were later delivered to The Major and his lieutenants, since we could no longer speak to Rinnan or Maltau. The letters were addressed to the Australian government, human rights organisations, the Australian public, the media, the United Nations — basically anyone we thought might listen. We simply wished for a new life far away from the militants and extremists who had haunted our lives. We came in peace.

These letters never reached the people they were addressed to. In any other situation, a formal letter requesting asylum would trigger a specified process. Shelter would be provided, and the relevant government agency tasked with processing the claim. But Canberra had skirted those obligations by ensuring the *Tampa* was pushed out of Flying Fish Cove, and that the SAS were stripped of any authority to receive asylum requests. This is also why Flying Fish Cove had been closed, and anyone who might have accepted such requests, such as police, lawyers, doctors and federal immigration officers, were prohibited from going near the *Tampa*. When media asked the Australian government about our claim for asylum, Canberra reinforced its commitment to the principle of non-refoulement. Asylum seekers had not been sent away, as the Australian government had never received a formal request for asylum in the first place.

Conditions in the square were worsening by the hour. The hunger strikers were frail and dropping like flies. Food and medical supplies had been sent from the island, but all was not as it seemed. For dinner one night we were served rice and chicken. I remember that Mum and I ate off the same disposable plate. It smelled slightly odd but we ate what was offered. Later that night almost everyone succumbed to a violent bout of food poisoning. The women and children especially began vomiting into buckets, plates, plastic bags. For what seemed like the millionth time in a week, I emptied my guts out. The latrines, already full, were emitting raw sewage across the square. I remember walking through other people's vomit and faeces to pee off the side of the ship. By the next morning conditions were worse on the *Tampa* than they had been aboard the *Palapa*.

AS THE *TAMPA* affair continued to dominate the news, a team of young lawyers at Liberty Victoria, a pro bono organisation in Melbourne, began to take notice. Listening to the prime minister's daily press briefings, they observed that Canberra was doing everything it could to deny the asylum seekers any legal representation and circumvent due process.

When Howard announced that he had commissioned the navy to tow the *Tampa* out into international waters, the lawyers scrambled. They began calling government officials, media outlets and human rights organisations, and eventually succeeded in reaching the *Tampa* by fax. The lawyers were willing to go to court to stop the expulsion of the *Tampa* but could not do so without a defendant. All they needed was one of our names. Rinnan hesitated, fearing that a legal battle would mire the shipping line in even murkier waters. Wilhelmsen HQ was also reluctant to engage in a legal battle. Speaking from Oslo, they were hopeful that a swift resolution could be brokered, and continued to insist that landing the survivors was the best course of action.

Undeterred, the lawyers would continue to mount a challenge.

DAY 9, FRIDAY 31 AUGUST

Before the sun rose on the last day of August, Ove Thorsheim, Norwegian ambassador to Australia, landed on Christmas Island. Oslo had sent him with a stern order to resolve the dispute and figure out exactly why Canberra was holding the Norwegian vessel hostage. The SAS kept him away from the *Tampa* for the entire morning while they awaited a green light from Canberra. Also held up at Flying Fish Cove were members of the Red Cross, ready with legal and medical assistance, as well as interpreters fluent in Farsi. The Australian government was playing a high-stakes game.

Eventually the prime minister's office granted permission to Ambassador Thorsheim to come aboard, but not the Red Cross.

Rinnan came down from the bridge to welcome the ambassador. It was the first time most of us had actually seen the captain. Throughout this whole ordeal he was a silver-haired figure in the sky, almost like a figment of our imagination. And now here he stood: a short, stout man with deep wrinkles and a furrowed brow. The two men shook hands and Rinnan walked the ambassador through the square, with The Major following.

None of us knew who this tall man was, but they spoke the same language. One of our delegation pleaded in broken English with them both to bring an end to the situation.

Another man rushed towards Thorsheim, holding out a scrunched piece of paper.

'Please, save us,' he pleaded to the ambassador.

The Major stepped in, snatching the paper before Thorsheim could read it. Thorsheim and Rinnan shook their heads and continued their inspection before heading to the bridge.

Some moments later, The Major brought them back the letter, having received an okay from Canberra. The letter was written in English and Thorsheim read it. Just as he had expected, it was a request for asylum:

> *Respected Australian government and gentlemen and ladies. You know well about the long time war and its tragic human consequences, and you know about the genocide and massacres going on in our country and thousands of men, women and children were put in public graveyards and we hope that you understand that keeping in view all aforementioned reasons we have no way but to run out of our dear homeland and to seek a peaceful asylum.*

To Thorsheim, this was a game-changer. In his hand was

the one thing that Canberra could not dispute. Thorsheim refused to hand the letter back to the SAS and demanded to be taken back to shore. The SAS officer said this could not happen until he had the letter back, and so a routine meeting quickly became a diplomatic incident, where an Australian soldier, acting on orders, was denying free passage to an accredited Norwegian diplomat. Thorsheim remained on the bridge for the rest of the day as Oslo and Canberra butted heads. We last saw Thorsheim and Rinnan at sunset, when the diplomat had finally been given the approval to leave, letter in hand.

MEANWHILE, THE PRIME MINISTER of Nauru had signed his approval for the construction of the temporary processing centres. For the sum of AU$10 million, a single line item in AusAid's budget, the Australian government had got its way: it now had the land for its coveted offshore processing centre. More importantly, it had been agreed that while the centre would be on Nauruan soil, its operation would lie beyond the rule of the island's judiciary.

Canberra moved at lightning pace, commissioning anyone who could wield a hammer to get to the island and start building. Nine weeks before the country went to the polls, Howard had assembled all of the puzzle pieces. Dubbed the 'Pacific Solution', it was what he needed to swing the election.

The New Zealand government, for its part, had made arrangements that would represent a turning point in my life. On the afternoon of Friday 31 August, Prime Minister Helen Clark telephoned John Howard to inform him that New Zealand would take up to 150 of the refugees, primarily women, children and families.

Unaware of Canberra's deal with Nauru, Clark hoped the offer would break the deadlock, which was spiralling into a diplomatic quagmire.

For our family it spelt a new life.

15.

THE PACIFIC SOLUTION

DAY 10, SATURDAY 1 SEPTEMBER

We had been aboard the *Tampa* for a whole week. With no possessions, we had been wearing the same clothes all this time. On top of the foul stench and the unbearable heat, we were bored to death, sitting cross-legged on the deck for much of the day with absolutely nothing to do, under the constant gaze of the soldiers.

After our breakfast of biscuits and juice, The Major came down for his usual update. Expecting the same old story, few of us were ready when he delivered some actual news.

'In a few days you will all be transferred to another ship. It is better, with beds and toilets. New Zealand has agreed to take some of you.'

An immediate barrage of questions broke out after these sentences were translated.

'Who is New Zealand?' one man asked.

'Where is he? Let me speak to him!' said another.

'What about everyone else? Where will the other ship take us?'

'Why will Australia not accept us?'

The Major patiently explained that New Zealand was a separate island nation close to Australia.

People were not convinced. No one had heard of New Zealand. Perhaps they were being tricked into getting off on some godforsaken island in the middle of nowhere. By now the level of trust was very low and the interrogation of The Major continued. He had come down to give us answers, but none of them had given any comfort.

At the next day's update, The Major announced that HMAS *Manoora* would be arriving tomorrow and taking us all on board. We were also told for the first time that our case was going to court in Australia. Lawyers from Liberty Victoria had got their hands on Thorsheim's letter and lodged a case with the Federal Court in Melbourne. What The Major did *not* tell us was that the lawyers acting for us had petitioned the court to request that we remain on the *Tampa* until the case was heard.

Had we known there was even the slimmest chance

of getting to Australia if we stayed aboard the *Tampa*, we would have refused to board the *Manoora*. As intolerable as conditions were on the *Tampa*, we had suffered for eleven days — what was a few more? But we knew nothing about the court petition. The Major also failed to mention that the *Manoora* would be headed to Nauru to offload those not going on to New Zealand. He simply told us the *Manoora* would be a much more comfortable ship for us while our case was being litigated.

We should have been thrilled at the thought of finally getting off the *Tampa*, but we were not. This was the devil we knew. Questions swirled throughout the square; no one trusted the Australian government by this point. We suspected their every move. What if they were taking us to prison? What if they were sending us back?

Back in Australia, John Howard was unveiling the second part of his masterplan. He called a press conference to announce that under his new 'Pacific Solution', all asylum seekers would be sent to processing centres offshore, beginning with Nauru. Ever the slick communicator, Howard presented this as a humane policy, and welcomed the support of the international community. The announcement was met with wide public support; talkback radio was filled with vehement calls to turn back the boats at all costs. Very few had any awareness of the lengths Canberra had gone to to stop the *Tampa*.

Our last day aboard the *Tampa* began with our usual prayer, and soon after, a ship dotted the horizon. In a reminder of the day the *Tampa* had approached the *Palapa*, this ship steamed towards us as we watched. It was a sleek, angular vessel, with a deck at either end and a large tower in the middle. HMAS *Manoora* was a 160-metre troopship that had just finished a deployment to the Solomon Islands.

It arced its way around Christmas Island and neared the *Tampa*. From atop the cliffs on the island a journalist took a photo that became another one of very few authorised illustrations for the story.

A hatch at the back of the *Manoora* opened and an empty barge launched into the water, heading towards the *Tampa*. We had lived in the 'town square' for seven days and it was now time to leave. We were led along one side of the *Tampa*, past the bridge and down several flights of stairs through a metal labyrinth. Once we reached the back of the ship at sea level, a gate rolled up, revealing the sea, and the barge waiting to take us to the *Manoora*.

We had been a remarkably united group to this point, but divisions started to show now. We had been told New Zealand would only accept families and children. While that provided some relief and certainty for my family and others like us, it was excruciating for everyone else – all those who, in leaving their families behind, had arguably sacrificed more than us.

Some of those men now refused to leave the *Tampa*. The Major employed his most soothing tone to make the *Manoora* sound attractive, promising beds, showers and fresh food. With the most recalcitrant, he was more direct. If they did not willingly board the *Manoora* they would be taken by force. The only ones to remain behind were the captain and crew of the *Palapa*.

There was to be no goodbye to Captain Rinnan. Throughout the whole ordeal we had seen him only the once. We wanted to thank him for his bravery. Had it not been for him, this story would have ended before it began. He and his crew had done an incredible job in the circumstances. I will never forget the bubble bath that healed my skin. Or Maltau shaving our heads that first day.

Rinnan and the crew would later be applauded by the international community for their bravery. One citation for an award from the United Nations stated that Rinnan had 'demonstrated personal courage and a unique degree of commitment to refugee protection'. His citation for International Shipmaster of the Year read: 'He and his Officers were able to recognise and to cope courageously and admirably with the desperation of the Refugees and with the SAS Commando Force sent onboard by the Australians.'

To this day, I am grateful for their courage, humanity and warm hospitality.

As well as giving us shelter, the *Tampa* lent its name to a story that will live forever. I do not wish to sleep in a container ever again.

THE BARGE RIDE to the *Manoora* took only a few minutes — short enough to ensure the dreaded seasickness did not return. The barge went back and forth, ferrying groups of about twenty at a time. It was as if a big red bird was coughing up food to feed its small grey chick.

The barge discharged us in the rear hangar, a windowless garage used to store tanks and other armaments but currently empty. From there we were led to the helideck, where we were photographed and given numbered lanyards. From the helideck we took one last look at the *Tampa*, its red hull piercing the horizon.

After having our photos taken, we were ushered back down to the hangar. This huge grey metal rectangle, big enough to house multiple large vehicles, would be our new town square. When the hatch was shut, it looked just like a giant container. Where were the beds, showers and fresh food? In announcing the news of the *Manoora*, Howard had claimed that we would be using the same facilities as the crew, but this was not to be the case. We were held in the hangar for containment. Along one side of the hangar were rows of stretchers, each with a blanket and pillow. There were not enough for everyone, so priority was given to the women and children. Our family set up camp in one corner with the other families, and for the first time in two weeks I lay on something other than timber or metal.

We heard later that as soon as we were out of sight, the Australian Federal Police boarded the *Tampa* and took the crew of the *Palapa* into custody. Major Khan and the SAS were the last to leave the *Tampa*, gifting Rinnan a plaque commemorating the events of the past week before joining us on the *Manoora*. As the *Manoora* headed away from Christmas Island, the *Tampa* was finally allowed to berth in Flying Fish Cove. Rinnan, Maltau and the crew were welcomed by locals with drinks and fireworks.

They did not stay the night. After the drama of the past eight days, they wanted to get the hell out of there. Who could blame them?

THE *MANOORA* WAS a very different beast to the *Tampa*. On the *Tampa* we burned and blistered under the hot sun. Now we missed the light, as we were kept in the enclosed hangar the whole time. The gentle ocean breeze was replaced by the deafening noise of the engine. The smell of sewage was replaced by diesel fumes. We had no way of telling if it was day or night.

The crew brought a large bin full of donated clothes destined for the Solomon Islands. We were also given a toothbrush and a towel each. I will never forget my first shower. We had two minutes before the water was cut off, but in that time I scrubbed myself clean of the filth that had caked my skin. I felt like one of those lizards in Sungjoy, drinking in the warmth of the sun and shedding my skin. I dried myself with the clean, dry towel and put on a pair of red shorts and a T-shirt that Mum had picked for me from the clothes bin. At some point on the *Palapa* I had lost my sandals. When I finally wore socks over my blistered feet, it felt like I was walking on clouds.

Food was rationed more tightly than on the *Tampa*, with meals usually no more than one piece of fruit or a slice of bread. Realising that the battle had been lost, hunger strikers broke their fast. They began taking water in small sips, and morsels of food.

The Major was on board and he and the crew, dressed in their smart navy uniforms, conducted the daily briefs. The next day The Major welcomed aboard officials from

the intergovernmental International Organisation for
Migration (IOM) and Immigration New Zealand (INZ),
as well as some Farsi-speaking translators. These officials
had been sent to determine who among us would go
to New Zealand and who would stay on Nauru. They
set up a table on one side of the hangar and asked us
to sit as family units. Like pieces of a jigsaw puzzle, we
sat in different parts of the hangar, our lanyards around
our necks.

The officials were patient as they took down all our
names and connected the dots in our stories. Having
worked with refugees, they were well versed in the plight
of the Hazara. Through a translator, Dad retold our story
while the officials took notes and filled out an endless stack
of forms. This process continued for much of the day.

People cried as they talked about being widowed,
orphaned or separated from their families. For a group
of solo teenagers this questioning proved especially
harrowing as they had to describe how their fathers had
been killed or disappeared at the hands of the Taliban.
Being of military age, many of these boys had left their
families when the Taliban overran Bamiyan and Mazar-e-
Sharif. Some had spent years in refugee camps in Pakistan
before finally deciding on the Australia route. Others had
been homeless or in detention centres across Indonesia

for almost a year before the *Palapa*. These 'Tampa boys' had not been in touch with their families for years. They provided names of family members in the slim hope that they might still be alive.

THE DAYS ABOARD the *Manoora* seemed to blend into one endless grey span. Today I don't recall a lot of detail, but some incidents have stayed in my mind.

The only meal that I remember involved chilli. Early into our voyage the chefs had prepared a rice and curry dish. We lined up as usual, and before those at the back of the queue had even picked up their trays, the people at the front who had begun to eat their meal began to gasp as if they were choking. Grown men began to sweat and tear up as children screamed as if they had been burned. The dish turned out to have been laced with industrial quantities of chilli. No one touched any food for the rest of the day.

People I interviewed for this book were in two minds about the incident. Was it a cruel prank on a bunch of desperate asylum seekers, like the jam incident on the *Tampa*, or did the chefs decide they would oblige our Middle Eastern taste buds with a little reminder of home cuisine?

Another day a crew member wheeled in a big black box with a window. It was the first time most of the children, including myself, had seen a television. We stared at the moving display of people in colourful outfits singing and dancing in a language we didn't understand. Years later I would see those same characters again — they were the Wiggles. That television became a fixture for the rest of the voyage, opening our eyes to the colourful world of the *Teletubbies* and other children's shows. With our eyes glued to the screen, we would teleport away from the cold grey hangar.

As the INZ and IOM officials processed our documents, they also advocated on our behalf with the crew. Major Khan had at some stage been replaced by a more amenable man named Major Dunn, and the officials told him we needed sunlight and fresh air. About ten days since we had left the *Tampa*, we once again felt the sun and wind on our faces. Twice a day, in small groups, we were allowed to sit on the helidecks at the bow and stern of the *Manoora*. I remember on one of our first excursions, Shekufah became seasick. A crew member rushed to get a plastic bag but got back a split-second too late: Shekufah sprayed that morning's breakfast on the sailor's crisp uniform.

WHILE WE ADJUSTED to our new existence, the world outside changed forever. It was 11 September 2001 —

9/11. Everyone remembers where they were and what they were doing that day. Unlike many, we did not see the horrifying images of New York's Twin Towers coming down, nor did we understand its true impact on the world. Major Dunn delivered the news to us in one of the usual morning briefings. We wondered mostly what it would mean for Afghanistan and our asylum claims. Were we still the asylum seekers we had been yesterday, or were we now a threat to national security? Would the rest of the world equate us with the very people we were fleeing from?

As a child, I had even less sense of the gravity of the situation. It is only in hindsight that I wonder how the asylum seeker situation would have played out had 9/11 not happened.

As we languished on the *Manoora*, Liberty Victoria fought our case in the Federal Court of Australia. The lawyers argued that in preventing the *Tampa* rescuees from seeking asylum, the federal government had acted outside the scope of the Migration Act. Justices Beaumont and French ruled in favour of the government's actions, ruling that 'the rescuees were not detained by the Commonwealth or their freedom restricted by anything that the Commonwealth did'. However, Chief Justice Black dissented, stating that the government had overstepped the parameters of the executive. '[T]here was a detention [of the asylum seekers by the Commonwealth government] . . . and that since it was not justified by the powers conferred by the Parliament under the Migration Act it was not justified by law.'

As television screens displayed the drama of the ADF carrying out 'Operation Relex', the general public had little awareness of the court battle, or the lengths the government had gone to cover its tracks. Justice Black's words would prove prophetic, however, as the conduct of the Howard government would pave the way for an executive-led detention policy that is still in place today. In the shadow of the 9/11 terrorist attacks, Australia's Border Protection Act came into force, shielding the government from any legal challenges to the action of processing asylum seekers offshore.

IT WAS AT this point that we first heard the name Nauru.

'The *Manoora* will take you to Nauru. The Australian government will process your claims for asylum there.' Major Dunn delivered the news to the English speakers of our group. Many had given up hope by now. We had been at sea for nearly a month, and for some, the idea of land — any land — seemed preferable to this.

For the families and the '*Tampa* boys' it was a different story. After a stopover on Nauru, we would be heading for a new life in New Zealand.

16.
DAY 35

THE *MANOORA* DROPPED anchor a few kilometres from Nauru, and a barge was used to transport small groups at a time. This process took several days because many were still suspicious of the Australian government's motivations and reluctant to go ashore. Major Dunn assured them the processing centres provided accommodation facilities of the highest quality. They would be staying in private air-conditioned rooms while their claims were being processed. As previously, if they refused to leave they would be forced. In the absence of any choice, a group of the men bid us farewell.

I hugged the man who had given me the candy on the *Palapa*. I wondered if I would ever see him again.

A media throng awaited these men. For the first time

since the *Tampa* had appeared in newspapers and on the nightly television news, the outside world could finally put some faces to the story. They were questioned on how they felt about 9/11. With little English, the men expressed their sympathy for the victims and explained that they themselves were fleeing from the perpetrators.

They were bussed from the shore to the 'prime hotel rooms' they had been promised. In the three weeks since the *Manoora* had left Christmas Island, the Australian government had flown scores of contractors to Nauru. They had arrived to a barren patch of land on the site of a former phosphate mine and set to erecting dozens of tents in neat rows, surrounding them with a razor-wire fence. This was the offshore processing centre Howard had been proud to declare open for business.

Upon seeing the makeshift prison the first group stopped in their tracks, only to be herded behind the wire. With no idea of what awaited them, the rest followed and met the same fate. Of the 433 asylum seekers who had boarded the *Palapa*, 302 men became the first inmates of Australia's first offshore detention centre.

We were in the last group to come ashore. The hangar was almost empty now and the crew seemed a little more relaxed. While parents talked eagerly about what the future held, we watched a final episode of *Teletubbies*. Having been sheltered, fed and watered for the past three weeks, we had a bit more colour in our faces, and some meat on our bones. The ulcers, sunburn, skin lesions, headlice and diarrhoea were gone. We were ready for the next chapter of our journey.

The cargo doors at the stern of the *Manoora* slowly opened like a drawbridge. It struck me that besides the water seeping into the *Palapa*, this was the closest we had come to touching the sea since we had left Indonesia. Many chose to wade through the water lapping at the ramp, a small act of rebellion against the infinite ocean that had been a darkness bearing down on our minds for the past month.

The crew were there for the farewell, adjusting our life-jackets and doing their best to calm the children unnerved by the noise of the machinery. In all our time aboard the *Manoora*, my family had not one single bad experience with the crew. They were strict and brusque at times, but generally attentive to our needs, even if we could not talk to each other because of the language barrier. We understood they were simply doing their job, and many sympathised with our situation.

We drew up to a small wharf jutting out into the shallow lagoon and stepped off the barge gingerly. So close to salvation, no one wanted to drown in a few inches of water at the last hurdle. A crowd of locals swarmed around us and we were surprised to see short, stout brown folks who did not look too different to us. They wore colourful shirts, and draped floral necklaces around our necks as we boarded a waiting bus. As the bus climbed up the dirt road to the airport, I gazed out to sea. It was the last time we would see the *Manoora*. Five months later it would arrive in the Persian Gulf as part of Australia's commitment to the War on Terror.

We waited in a little hall by the airstrip, being fed some biscuits and bottles of water. IOM officials handed out last-minute documents and treats for the children — I remember being given a pair of bright blue plastic jandals. By now, we had formed a tight-knit group. Parents shared stories of the last 35 days at sea, while we children became best friends. Atayee and Dad had become close over the last few weeks, and both were fathers of five. Atayee doted on Mojtaba, who the nurses concluded had contracted malaria, probably while we were in Jakarta. During the last 48 hours aboard the *Manoora*, we were told that the families would leave on two flights, one day apart, with seating organised alphabetically. Realising he had been placed on the first flight, Atayee had asked officials to ensure that our seats be swapped, as Mojtaba had still not recovered. Through a clerical error, this did not eventuate, leaving us on the *Manoora* for an extra day, something which still sticks with Atayee. There are countless other acts of kindness and community among our group, and we would rely on these forged bonds heavily in the years to come.

As we waited for the plane that would take us to our new home, sadness filled the room. We had no idea what had happened — or would happen — to the men of our group, many of whom we had got to know. We felt incredibly lucky to be going to New Zealand. We knew nothing about that country, but it had to be better than this barren rock in the middle of the ocean.

IN FACT, THE men would remain in detention on Nauru for more than three years before being eventually resettled, many of them in New Zealand. But for now they had no notion of that; they were trapped in the same limbo as those in Indonesia and Pakistan and elsewhere. Australia's offshore detention centres are designed to break the spirit of desperate people like us. At the time of writing, seventeen people have lost their lives in these centres through suicide or mistreatment, with dozens more in detention centres on the mainland. These in addition to countless self-harm attempts, including self-immolation, hanging, cutting and hunger strikes. Severe mental distress has also been documented among people languishing in these open-air prisons.

More than 4200 asylum seekers, men, women and children have spent some time on Australia's offshore processing centres. At its peak in 2014, the detention centres in Nauru and Manus Island were hosting more than 1200 and 1350 asylum seekers respectively. Those numbers have dwindled in recent years, as various governments in Canberra have tried everything except granting asylum to Australia. As of March 2021, there were 239 asylum seekers in offshore detention and a further 1000 on the mainland. Successive New Zealand governments have offered to accept up to 150 asylum seekers from offshore detention – an offer that has consistently been rejected by Canberra since it was first made in 2013.

Offshore detention costs Australian taxpayers 50 times more than what it would cost to let asylum seekers live in the community while their refugee claims are assessed. The Australian federal budget has regularly allowed for more than AU\$1 billion annually for offshore detention – more than 30 times greater than the country's contribution to UNHCR – and more than AU\$12 billion since 2012 alone. It would be cheaper to house every asylum seeker currently held in detention in individual homes across Sydney's most desirable suburbs and pay them a matching salary, than it is to continue to fund the current scheme. It is confounding that the same governments that stress fiscal prudence are willing to spend billions of taxpayer dollars to imprison and torture a specific group of people. Years from now we will look back on this episode as a shameful blight on Australian history, a stain on the country's reputation. Sadly, by the time a commission of inquiry is ordered into this policy, the perpetrators will long be dead. It's likely no one will be held accountable for this flagrant disregard for human rights and international law, or the misery and suffering inflicted on those who ventured in search of a better life.

I was one of the lucky ones. If we had not been saved by New Zealand's generosity, my life would have been very different.

17.

LAND OF THE

LONG WHITE

CLOUD

WE LANDED IN New Zealand on 28 September 2001, six months after we had boarded that lorry out of Sungjoy. After a brief stopover in Fiji, we landed at Auckland airport. Each family was taken to an interview room with customs and immigration officials. My parents were grilled on every detail. The officials were courteous and professional, and there was a translator present. We had arrived at sunrise and it was late in the afternoon when we were finally released.

In a twist of fate, the first American troops had landed in Afghanistan on the very day we landed in New Zealand, kicking off another episode in the graveyard of empires. A dozen CIA agents carrying US$10 million in cash met with remaining members of the Northern Alliance, laying the groundwork for a US invasion in the following weeks.

The bus carrying us from Auckland Airport to the nearby Mangere Refugee Resettlement Centre had its curtains drawn in case there were protesters. But no one came to protest against our arrival in New Zealand; instead, we were met with a song and dance and more food than I had ever seen.

The first thing that struck me about New Zealand was the greenery. We had arrived in spring when everything seemed to be bursting with life. Dad joked how we were like sheep and cows in a wide-open field, surrounded by vivid green bushes, lush grass, fresh air and the best water we had ever tasted.

Mangere marked a number of firsts for all of us, introducing us to new customs, new language, new sights, sounds and tastes — a whole new world of dreams and opportunities.

For Mum and Dad it was an especially poignant time. Neither had ever received any formal education; though, as mentioned previously, Dad learnt to read and write Farsi while working in Iran. As a young girl in Afghanistan, Mum, like so many others, never learnt to read or write. Even though she could speak fluent Farsi, she had never written her own name. When we received

our identification cards at Mangere we all had to sign for
them. Mum, who had never been asked for a signature
in her whole life — who did not even understand the
significance of owning a distinctive mark of one's name —
shakily marked the paper with an X.

Our days at Mangere were structured. After weeks in
limbo, we found comfort in routine and organisation.
Following a communal breakfast at the dining hall
we would go to our respective classes. All the children,
regardless of age, were in one class as we were all new to
learning English. I remember walking into the classroom
for the first time and instantly feeling as if I had been
transported to the future. There were neat rows of desks
and chairs and all the stationery you could dream of. The
cold dirt floor of the school I'd attended briefly in Jaghuri
was replaced by carpet in an insulated room, its walls
decorated with colourful paintings, posters and photos.
A map of the world had a landmark highlighted on each
country — a statue of a robed green woman holding a torch
in America, a tall triangular tower in France, an orange
rock in Australia.

The largest area was dedicated to something called
Kiwiana, with a giant map of New Zealand surrounded
by photos of kiwifruit, kiwi, jandals, bees, trees, beaches,
marae and pōhutukawa. The artworks were beautiful —

intricate patterns, like rolling waves or clouds, which we would learn later were called koru. We learnt where we were in the country, and traced our fingers right across the map from Afghanistan, to Pakistan, to Indonesia, across the Indian and Pacific oceans, and finally to New Zealand, tucked away at the bottom.

We were such a long way from home.

It was at Mangere that I learnt the alphabet. I learnt about small and capital letters, and that the sentence 'The quick brown fox jumps over the lazy dog' contains every letter. I learnt to count using an abacus and laughed at how the word sounded like Abbas. We would all giggle when someone forgot their own name mid-sentence because their tongues were twisting around foreign words. I learnt greetings and would use them at every opportunity – to the teachers, the receptionists, the security guards, the cooks in the kitchen. By the end of our time at Mangere, I would string together several sentences with scant regard for grammar or structure. 'Hello my name is Abbas and I am from Afghanistan and I like football and Ali is my brother and I like food and my Dad is Abdul and my Mum is Goldastah and I am hungry.'

We just soaked it all up. We were kids again and I was unstoppable. The ladies in the kitchen took a shine to this chubby little kid with an attitude. They often gave me an extra serving of whatever was on the menu. I credit my rapid growth at that time to the lavish amounts of New Zealand meat, milk and cheese that were the staple of our two months at Mangere.

Dad was eager to catch up on all that had happened while we were at sea. The Taliban had assassinated Ahmad Shah Massoud, the last commander of the Northern Alliance, two days before the 9/11 attacks. We were horrified at the scale and brazenness of the attacks and knew that the world had changed forever. Through BBC Farsi, our parents listened to US president George Bush discuss his decision to invade Afghanistan.

We welcomed the removal of the Taliban and knew that our country would never be the same again. We also learnt of the lengths Australia had gone to deny us permission to disembark on its territory. We watched as John Howard won the election, only weeks after pushing one of the most egregious pieces of fake news during a modern election, that the asylum seekers 'irresponsibly sank the damn boat, which put their children in the water'.

But perhaps the most horrible news was the sinking of what became known as SIEV X. Just like the *Palapa*, it was heavily overloaded with more than 400 asylum seekers, most of them fleeing Iraq. It had been caught in a storm, and sunk in international waters between the Indonesian island of Java and Christmas Island, not far from where the *Palapa* had been rescued. SIEV X claimed the lives of 353 people, the majority of them women and children. Seeing the distressing images of the wreckage, we realised how close we had come to certain death. That could have been us.

AT SCHOOL WE learnt about life in New Zealand. The country's history and the importance of Māoridom. We learnt basic rules of life, such as the emergency services number, individual rights and responsibilities. Above all else we were given simple lessons on how to thrive in our new lives. I look back at our time in Mangere with fond memories. It was a fantastic orientation to life in New Zealand.

Towards the end of our stay at Mangere, our group dwindled as we began to move out to permanent housing throughout New Zealand. While some families would be staying in Auckland, many of us were sent to Christchurch. We knew there would be many challenges ahead, but we felt well-equipped for the next chapter. As we packed our dormitories on that final day, I thought back to how every move before had been rushed and secretive. That day, we all took our time to embrace our neighbours, thank the generous staff, and take a deep breath.

PARADISE WAS A state house on Ballantyne Avenue in Upper Riccarton, with a white picket fence, a vibrant green front yard, a fireplace complete with a brick chimney, and a cream weatherboard exterior. Every family had a team of volunteers pick them up from the airport, everyday Kiwis who had replied to a Red Cross advertisement in the local paper. They had received some training from Refugee and Migrant Services (RMS), an agency that would be a critical support for us over the next few years. Half a dozen volunteers had been assigned to the Nazari clan. There was Ola, Gavin, Prue, Colin and our favourites, Chris and Jan. These volunteers would become an integral part of our lives. On that first journey our volunteers drove us along Memorial Avenue to Ilam Road, to Church Corner and finally to Ballantyne Ave, a tree-lined street with a row of neat houses set back from the road.

Walking through the blue front door into our new home was like emerging from underwater and taking a huge gulp of air. I marvelled at the hallway, the windows, the wallpaper, the weird appliances in the kitchen, the beds, chairs and tables that filled in the rooms. So much furniture! We were a long way from our thatched roof mudbrick homestead in Sunjoy. I can only imagine what it must have been like for my parents.

Perhaps my favourite spot in the whole house was a

shed in the back yard, which housed more books than I had ever seen. Boxes and boxes of books were stacked along the walls, and beneath items of donated gardening furniture. Over the years, I would read almost every book in that shed.

More than six months after boarding up our life in Sungjoy and climbing into the back of a truck with one trunk of belongings between us, we were beginning life anew. This was our new home and everything was going to be all right. Our volunteers had even arranged for our first meal to be a little reminder of the home we had left — we feasted on rice and lamb qorma.

A diverse, working-class community, Upper Riccarton was the perfect landing spot. My first interaction with Kiwi kids was with the other boys on our street. Ballantyne Ave was home to Pākehā, Polynesian, Māori and Asian families, with plenty of boys our age. There were the Mo'ungas, the Tagicakibaus, the Fetus, the Nguyens, and the van Noordens. In Sungjoy I had been surrounded by others who walked, talked and looked like me. I didn't know what to expect, and wondered what I would have in common with these other children, who all looked so different.

I needn't have worried. We quickly became friends as we all walked to and from Riccarton Primary School.

We would all bike around the cul-de-sac. When it rained, the drains would become blocked and the entire street would flood, creating a little pool to splash through. We would throw a ball around the local park or chase one another in the playground. We would walk to and from school together, with a detour to the local dairy most days. Some of those friendships are still going strong today.

Looking back on those times, I am so grateful for the childhood we had, because it shaped my view of New Zealand. We had arrived at a point in time when New Zealand was becoming a more diverse country, and our neighbourhood showcased that diversity. We were the first Middle Eastern family in the street, Mum's and Shekufah's headscarves attracted the odd second glance, but by and large we felt at peace. Each passing day and experience strengthened our sense of belonging.

'GREEN MEANS GO. Orange means slow. Red means no. That's all you need to know,' said Jan. A valuable lesson in how not to get killed on the roads. When we left Sungjoy there was not one installed traffic light in the whole of Afghanistan. I stared with growing anticipation as the red man blinked and finally turned green.

'Everything is so orderly here,' exclaimed Dad. 'It's incredible.'

The weekly benefit payment we received was not a nice round number, but calculated to the last cent. Prices at the supermarket added up precisely, and exact change was given. There was no room for haggling. At first Dad often took a calculator to ensure that the checkout operator wasn't ripping him off.

Everything ran to time. We were amazed at the detailed timetables at every bus stop and Dad would check the accuracy of every bus arrival on his watch; almost all were accurate to within a minute.

'See how a functioning society operates, son? No dramas. They just get on with it. This is how it should be. We need to do the same.'

But Dad was also acutely aware of how far we had to go, and frequently reminded us. He employed a number of analogies that he felt captured our situation.

'We are in debt,' he would remind us. 'We are not even at ground level. We are starting from below ground and must work twice as hard to get out.'

'We have many red lights in front of us,' Dad would say. 'But every red eventually turns green, and if you time it right you might get a run of green lights all the way.'

We felt like babies learning to walk. We crawled, then

took hesitant steps, constantly falling down. Language remained the biggest barrier: we were heavily dependent on Jan and the other volunteers for the first few months. But then we picked up pace. We children were enrolled at Riccarton Primary School, and Mum and Dad attended English lessons at the Pacific Education and Employment Training Organisation (PEETO), a government-funded training and employment centre. Every night we gathered around the fireplace, all of us doing our homework. At school we were all placed in the ESOL class (English for speakers of other languages), and were tested monthly. Within six months our English was good enough for us to graduate from ESOL and enter mainstream classrooms with everyone else.

As refugees, we had been victims to powerful forces outside our control. But Dad ensured that we never allowed the thought of our struggle to influence our new lives. Any notion of victimhood disappeared when we arrived in Christchurch. Dad would remind us that Afghanistan ranked at the bottom of the world in every social metric, be it health, education or equality of opportunity. He would joke that Afghanistan would only rank first if the list was in alphabetical order. Being resettled to the bottom of the world was a tectonic shift in our lives. We now had everything we needed to thrive. Opportunity was a charging bull, and it was up to us to wrestle it by the horns. Realising where we had come from gave us an incredible perspective. We knew the task of rebuilding our lives would not be easy. But we felt empowered, with an urgency to improve our lot. Dad had risked it all to provide a better future for his family and he had brought us all the way. It was time to wrestle the bull.

WE SOON FELL into a routine of work, school and play. During those early years, this is what a usual week looked like in the Nazari household.

During the week us children attended school, while every morning Mum and Dad went to their English classes. Dad would spend the afternoons labouring on construction sites, or finding odd jobs to keep busy. Mum would go to pick up Mojtaba and Mostafa, the latest addition to our family, from kindergarten and prepare a meal in time for us when we got home from school. Ali, Sakhi and I would wolf it down before heading off to after-school sports. We boys all took a liking to football and joined the local club, Avon United FC. We particularly liked the oranges at half-time.

At thirteen, Shekufah had only one year of primary school to go before she would start high school. Her mind was firmly set on improving her education prospects, so after school most days she went to the local library. Her efforts paid off and she was selected as an out-of-zone student for Burnside High School, paving the way for the rest of us to follow in her footsteps.

The weekends were always packed. Mum and Dad spent Saturday mornings traipsing around garage sales and farmers' markets while we were at football, and Shekufah babysat Mojtaba and Mostafa. Then we would spend the afternoons going somewhere together. One of my favourite destinations was the public library in the central city. We would bus into town, return our books and take out a whole lot more.

We took every opportunity to familiarise ourselves with Christchurch. We climbed to the spire of Christchurch Cathedral, looking down at the buskers in Cathedral Square. We splashed in the fountains of Hagley Park and strolled through the Botanic Gardens.

One of my favourite parts of the Gardens was the area near the museum. Mum would push Mostafa in the pram and we played around near the colourful flowers. It was easy to see why Christchurch was called the Garden City.

Mum had a penchant for picnics — she would create a decadent feast and pack it into chilly bins. We would choose a spot, usually a piece of neatly cut grass under a tree, and there we would unpack the heady menu of Afghan food. As we grew more accustomed to New Zealand food, we added fish and chips to our menu.

Mum and Dad spent every Sunday morning at the Riccarton Market, a huge weekly event organised by the local Rotary Club and held on the grounds of a racecourse. To this day, the market remains one of Dad's favourite places. They would get there as early as possible in the day, with Dad on the lookout for gardening equipment or anything else that took his fancy. Once he had eyed up something he wanted, his Afghan instincts would kick in. How much, he would ask? Oh, too expensive. To him, this was like the bazaars of Afghanistan — much more expensive, but cleaner and safer. Mum would make a beeline for the honey and wool stalls, buying up industrial-size jars of organic honey from local apiarists, and woollen socks and cardigans from sheep farmers.

Australia rarely came to our thoughts now. Apart from watching the adventures of the Crocodile Hunter and Kath and Kim, we didn't have much of a connection to Australia. We were busy building a life in New Zealand.

IN THOSE FIRST years we were invited to sports tournaments, cultural festivals and all sorts of events organised by community groups such as RMS. For the adults there were often workshops offering career advice, financial planning, and tips on how to access social services. All these initiatives were incredibly beneficial in helping us navigate those early years.

Our learning journey was accelerated by an after-school programme called the Homework Club. Dad heard about it through his English tutor at PEETO, and I well recall my first session there. Ali, Sakhi, Shekufah and I got home from school one day and Dad announced that he wanted to take us somewhere to help with our homework. It was a cold winter evening and the sun had already set when we arrived at the majestic grounds of Hagley College. Dad had written down the room number and we followed the signs to a classroom on the upper floor of the main building. We walked into a classroom of empty desks and chairs, and a couple of teachers chatting to each other. Their eyes lit up as they saw us at the door.

'We are looking for the Homework Club,' I said hesitantly. 'Is this it?'

'Yes! Welcome!' said one of the tutors. 'You are the first ones here. We were beginning to think no one was going to show up!'

The tutors invited us to sit down and take out our homework. Within minutes I was learning about compound words. Ali was learning about fractions, while Shekufah and Sakhi worked on book reviews. Dad stayed for the whole evening, sitting quietly at the back of the room. It was such an enjoyable couple of hours, and we had the entire place — and the tutors — to ourselves. The evening finished with juice and biscuits.

As we packed up to leave, one of the tutors handed Dad an envelope containing petrol vouchers. She thanked us for attending and encouraged us to come back next week — and invite all of our friends. On the way home we filled up the car with petrol using the vouchers.

That night Dad marvelled at our situation. Almost exactly a year after leaving Sungjoy, we were all healthy, housed and every one of us was receiving a full education. It was never lost on our parents how lucky we were. They saw education as the essential tool in making the most of our fresh start and fulfilling our potential.

The Hagley Homework Club was a mainstay of our education journey. We attended religiously, all through primary and well into high school. At the time of writing, the Homework Club is still going strong, twenty years after we walked through those doors. I offer my heartfelt thanks to the leadership of Hagley College for this initiative.

I WANT TO emphasise here that I strongly believe that children of immigrant and refugee backgrounds find it easier to learn and integrate into society when they are placed in a diverse community. The other essentials of course are a welcoming community and strong government support. If migrants coalesce in one area in large numbers, where they are encouraged to keep to themselves without exposure to other cultures, all sorts of social and economic challenges emerge. The burgeoning migrant neighbourhoods in many European countries are a case in point.

New Zealand takes in a relatively small number of refugees, for which it has been criticised. The recent increases to the refugee intake is a welcome step in changing the lives of a few lucky families. At the time of writing, INZ was trialling a community sponsorship scheme for refugees, modelled on the highly successful Canadian system. I hope this pilot scheme proves successful and becomes a permanent fixture of New Zealand's resettlement process. While I think there is further room to increase the quota, I believe New Zealand can take great pride in the generous and attentive service offered to those who are lucky to be granted entry. It is a comprehensive, wraparound service that includes housing, education and health services provided by the state, as well as a pathway to employment and the rights and responsibilities of citizenship. All of this is complemented by tailored support from a range of volunteers and community groups.

We had everything we needed in an environment in which we were afforded love, dignity and security. After so much instability, we now had a foundation upon which to rebuild anew. If our journey to New Zealand was us making it to the water's edge, then within a year we had jumped right in.

18.

WHOLE

AGAIN

MOSTAFA WAS BORN a year after we arrived in New Zealand. Mum was overjoyed to have another son, but his birth reminded us of Hussein, our eldest brother. As we started to fill the void of our new life, we began to feel more keenly that one puzzle piece was missing. The story of Hussein's journey to Iran is enough to fill a book on its own. Along with a handful of other teenagers he had sneaked across the border into Iran by night. He found work with some Afghans as a labourer, and even taught himself English.

We applied for a family reunification visa for Hussein but had no idea when − or if − it would be processed.

Hussein's absence weighed heavily on our family,

particularly on Mum. We weren't alone, either. A number of the *Tampa* families had a relative or two who had been left behind, or separated from them in one way or another. In 2004, as we neared the three-year residency requirement for Kiwi citizenship, we received the news that would finally make our family whole again.

Mum recalls receiving a formal-looking letter from Immigration New Zealand and clutching it tightly as she waited for us to return from school so we could translate it for her. Shekufah and Sakhi took turns reading it, to ensure they had understood each sentence properly before turning to Mum and Dad.

Hussein's family reunification visa had been approved!

Everything moved quickly after that. Hussein, along with several other *Tampa* relatives who had been accepted, was contacted by IOM and INZ officials. Hussein rushed around Iran pulling together his health records, finances, identification and other documentation, which, for a non-resident, proved a herculean task. Nevertheless, within a few months he was on a flight to Auckland. Hussein and the others also began their orientation in Mangere, sleeping in the same dorms that had housed us only three years earlier.

I could see Mum and Dad's mood improve by the day as Hussein completed his orientation and boarded a flight to Christchurch. Mum's name, Goldastah, means 'handful of flowers' and, true to her name, she put on her most colourful dress and headscarf for the occasion, carrying a bunch of flowers to greet her eldest son.

We gathered in the arrivals lounge, sitting with the other *Tampa* families, all brimming with excitement. One by one, families were reunited with their sons as they passed through customs. Hussein was the last to emerge, held up for a packet of dried mulberries. He looked older than his age, no doubt a sign of what he had endured.

Mum was over the moon — it was the happiest I had ever seen her. She held Hussein's hand the whole way home, as if he might vanish from our lives again if she let go. At home, Dad told us all what lay behind the reason he had sent Hussein abroad all those years ago. With the Taliban advancing into the highlands, it was clear that Hussein, being of military age, would be either killed or forced to join a militia. Dad knew that if the Taliban overran Sungjoy, it would be a bloodbath. He calculated that if we were all to perish, Hussein would be able to continue the family line.

A few months after Hussein's arrival, we became eligible for New Zealand citizenship. In May 2005 all the *Tampa* families in Christchurch were invited to the town hall for a special citizenship ceremony. Dressed in our best clothes, we stood for the national anthem. In my mind, we were already Kiwis, but for Dad the certificate was a sign of just how far we had come. Garry Moore, the mayor, gave a rousing speech in which he recalled how his Irish ancestors had faced persecution in England and in many other parts of the world. He remembered as a child being told about job advertisements that ended with 'NINA' – No Irish Need Apply. On top of that, the sectarianism between Catholics and Protestants had torn families apart for generations, including his own.

As newly minted Kiwis, the mayor said, the world was ours. He knew that, like any new arrivals, we carried baggage. Much of it was good, but a fair bit was useless – it weighed down our hearts and made the going tougher. In order to make the most of the opportunity before us, it was incumbent upon us to sort out which parts to keep and which parts to clear out.

Garry Moore's words still ring true to me, and his is a philosophy I apply to everything. Garry would become one of my mentors years later, and I have drawn on his wisdom to help me navigate life's many sticky points.

FOR THE 'TAMPA boys', the solo teenagers who had been accepted along with families, it had been a lonely few years. They were placed under the care of Child Youth and

Family, attending schools in Auckland and Christchurch while attempts were made to find their families. With the help of officials at INZ and IOM, they had managed to find their families scattered throughout Afghanistan, Iran and Pakistan. Many months and an astronomical phone bill later, the 'Tampa boys' were finally reunited with their families.

For the men sent to Nauru, it was a hellish experience. Trapped in a tent surrounded by razor wire fencing, they spent the days sleeping in the tropical sun, waiting for any news on their asylum claims. After more than three years on the island, the first groups of men were finally allowed to leave Nauru. Many were resettled to New Zealand, with a handful being accepted by Australia. Even though their lives had been put on hold for more than three years, they didn't skip a beat. Many immediately got stuck into English classes and set about finding jobs. Three years later, they would eventually become New Zealand citizens, and apply to bring their families over. It was bittersweet, as they had not seen their families for more than six years. The men of the *Tampa* had been to hell and back so that their families didn't have to take the same path. Theirs is an incredible story of fear, fortitude and family. In time, they too would weave the strands of their lives into the fabric of New Zealand society.

THERE IS SO much to say about our early years in Christchurch, but in this chapter I want to share a few stories that demonstrate the kinds of challenges we faced, as well as the perseverance and support that helped us overcome them.

When Mostafa was about a year old and learning to walk, he reached out one day for the edge of a tablecloth, pulling down the cloth and the pot of tea Mum had just set on it. The boiling liquid showered Mostafa's little body and he screamed in pain. Remembering a parenting class at Mangere, Mum held her small son under the cold tap while Dad grabbed a towel.

They were so flustered they forgot the little English they had acquired, and how to call an ambulance. With all of us at school, they agonised about what to do; then, remembering the medical clinic our sponsors had enrolled us in, they rushed out the door, Mostafa wrapped in a towel and losing consciousness. They ran a kilometre down the road, through an alleyway and along the main road to Riccarton Clinic, bursting in through the door. Dad wordlessly handed Mostafa to the receptionist, who judged the situation fast enough to call a doctor and nurse, who leapt into action. Within minutes an ambulance was on its way, and Mum and Dad soon found themselves with Mostafa at Christchurch Hospital.

Mostafa was immediately admitted for emergency surgery, while Mum and Dad sat glumly in the waiting area. They contemplated some of the other things they had learnt at Mangere — specifically that the police could take away children who were being abused. Would this count as abuse? They agonised as they sat in the plastic hospital chairs, wondering if their last image of Mostafa would be one of their little boy screaming in pain. Adding to their anguish, a police officer appeared before them, with a doctor and a woman in civilian clothes. Mum and Dad guessed she must be the government official who would preside over their maltreatment case — until she opened her mouth to speak in fluent Farsi.

'Salam. My name is Rubina,' she said warmly. 'I am a translator. I can see you are distressed but please do not worry. I am here to help.'

A wave of relief washed over Mum and Dad, similar to what they felt stepping aboard the *Tampa*.

'The doctors say your boy has been through a lot but will heal fully if they remove a patch of skin from the baby's thigh and graft it onto his upper body. They wanted to consult you before performing this surgery.'

'Oh yes, of course, please go ahead!'

Rubina stayed with Mum and Dad throughout that afternoon while Mostafa was on the operating table. She called our sponsors to ensure someone would be there when we got home from school, and rang us in the evening. We spoke with Mum and Dad, who were still obviously very upset, and we were relieved they were not alone.

Rubina was a translator for Language Line, a government-funded service for immigrants, and in this situation she was the rudder of our ship. People like Rubina continually stepped in to help lift the veil of confusion for us in those early years. Whether it was sitting a driving test, attending parent–teacher interviews, or making and attending doctor's appointments, help was on call. Thinking back on those years, I shudder at the thought of trying to navigate the traps of New Zealand life without the guidance of people like Rubina.

I'M NOT SURE which member of the community first came across berry-picking, but it was an instant hit. Although raspberries were a different shape and taste to the mulberries we were all used to in Afghanistan, picking raspberries became a summer fixture for every *Tampa* family resettled in Christchurch. For about eight weeks during the school holidays, from mid-November to mid-January, we would wake up at the crack of dawn and wolf down some tea and biscuits for breakfast, before being driven by a friend about half an hour to the berry farm in Belfast.

We parked on the grass along the country road rather than in the carpark, so the car would be in the shade of a tree. We lined up outside the shed around 6.45 a.m., the kids playing with the chickens and sheep while the adults chatted among themselves. At 7 a.m. on the dot the shed doors rolled up and the workday began. We were each handed two trays, both loaded with a dozen empty plastic punnets, and off we'd go to into the raspberry fields. On a bumper day a dozen families would clear an entire field of 100 rows, each longer than a football pitch. Once every punnet was full, we would carry the trays back to the shed, register them under our picker number and collect two more empty trays to fill.

We stopped when the orders for the day had been met, usually around late afternoon. Then we lined up outside the shed, collected the day's wages and ate a shared lunch. Apart from the stinging nettles and the red hands from berry juice, my lasting memory of every berry-picking season is the shared lunches. Under the shade of a tree, my parents reminisced about how this felt exactly like harvesting wheat back in Sungjoy.

The summers we worked at the berry farm were formative for me. Under the sweltering Canterbury sun we laboured away with little complaint. As well as the money, we revelled in the dignity of the work. Here was something we could all do, working with our hands and the sweat of our brows to earn a living.

In fact so eager were we to work that most Afghan men in our group had at least two jobs, alongside their studies. After language classes in the morning they would work an afternoon shift at a supermarket, say, or in a warehouse stacking shelves, and then an evening shift driving taxis or delivering pizzas. We took pride in every achievement along the way — from graduating into a higher English class to acquiring a new endorsement on a driver's licence. These people who came from a country with so little paperwork quickly progressed to collecting every piece they could.

We picked berries for about seven or eight summers, using the money to supplement the benefit payments we received. It allowed us to take the first steps towards self-sufficiency, as people purchased taxis or work vans. The money we made during that first season was used to buy our first car, a rusty 1986 Mitsubishi Mirage stationwagon. It would become our *saraacha*, with Dad ferrying us to Homework Club, football training and everywhere in between. Mum learnt to drive behind the wheel of that car, and became one of the first women in the community to get her licence, acing the test on her first attempt.

WITHIN A YEAR of being resettled in Christchurch, some *Tampa* parents became concerned that their children were losing their Farsi, so they set up a formal teaching programme. The tutors at PEETO allowed us to use their facilities on Sunday afternoons, so we packed into several classrooms and spent the afternoon reciting poems and reading textbooks in Farsi.

Most of the resources we used had been emailed from Iran and mass-printed at a local stationery warehouse. We started learning about our own culture. Removed from the suffocating focus on religious subjects that dominated the Afghan curriculum at the time, our Sunday school in Christchurch focused on history, arts and culture. I first heard the Afghan national anthem at Sunday school, years after I first heard 'God Defend New Zealand'. I learnt about the 34 provinces of Afghanistan and what each was famous for — pomegranates from Paktia, grapes from Kandahar, textiles from Balkh, and the breathtaking natural scenery in Nuristan.

Dad would complement our Sunday lessons by setting tests and lessons a few times a week after we had finished our English homework. He couldn't do much to help us with English — we were learning it much more quickly than he and Mum were, as children always do — but he wanted to do something. He asked one of the PEETO teachers to print out the daily news headlines from BBC Farsi, then gave us the printouts to read, and asked us to tell him what each article was about. I remember we always tripped up on the Farsi version of English names, which just don't look or sound right. Gorge Push? Jirj Boosh? Ooooh – George Bush!

As much as I disliked having an extra day of school while my non-Afghan friends were out playing, I now realise the importance of keeping one's mother tongue alive. I am eternally thankful to the teachers at my Sunday school – and especially to my dad – for teaching me so much, and helping me learn to read and write in Farsi. It is a connection to my place of birth that I cherish deeply. How ironic that I had to move to the other side of the world to learn my mother tongue.

I LAUGH NOW when I recall the many things that were completely mysterious to us in the beginning. Like the way our mailbox would silently fill with letters and flyers and newspapers multiple times a week and we had no idea who was behind this devious act. We saved every one of the deliveries for weeks, not knowing its significance or what any of it meant until one of our sponsors noticed, and explained to us the concept of junk mail and the work of the postal service. In Afghanistan, messages were sent via word of mouth and rarely written down. Bazaars never had any sales that they would have to leaflet people about. Years later my first job would be doing a weekly paper run.

Another time we kept seeing our neighbours' kids floating up into the air from behind the fence. They seemed to be reaching impossible heights. What kind of magic lay on the other side? Sensing our curiosity, they invited us over one day and soon enough we were all flying — up and down on their trampoline. We had never seen such a wonderful thing! Some months later, our sponsors found a trampoline at a local garage sale and we spent an afternoon piecing it together. That old trampoline with its rusted springs was a source of joy for many years.

For Mum and Dad, those early years were a turbulent time of immense highs and dark lows. They marvelled at our progress, and how us kids just soaked up the culture and the language. But on more than one occasion I would come home to find Mum crying at the foot of the bed. She was incredibly homesick and felt like an alien in a strange land. She welcomed the generosity, friendship and support of her classmates, and the other women of the *Tampa*, but she dearly missed our little homestead.

I could tell that Dad felt the same, but, in true Afghan

fashion, he didn't show much emotion. He missed his role in the community, and the agency and freedom he had enjoyed as the family breadwinner. Now he found himself as a voiceless, unemployed student, living on welfare. Both my parents found their situations demoralising at times, and wondered if they could stay in New Zealand long term. Would we ever truly feel at peace here? Would we ever fully regain our agency and sense of purpose? Some days at the start it felt as if all we could see were red lights. The challenges seemed insurmountable.

Looking back on those tough times, I don't know how we would have come out the other side if we had not had others in the community to lean on. The *Tampa* families in Christchurch drew strength from one another, and the weight seemed lighter because it was shared. Some weekends the families would meet up at a local park for a picnic. The adults would set up under a tree and talk, while we children would run around and play. It was comforting to know that, whatever challenges we faced in making sense of our new community, we were not alone.

In hindsight, I would not trade those experiences for anything. They instilled in us the value of hard work, and of just getting on with it. There were plenty of red lights, and those initial years were tough, but we stuck to it. One foot in front of the other.

Gradually, the texture of our daily existence began to change. Soon, the road became smooth, and before long we seemed to be catching every green light.

19.

THE KIWI DREAM

BY THE LATE 2000s we had been buoyed by a seemingly endless run of good fortune. While the early years seemed to go by at a snail's pace, the next decade flew by.

In 2006 we moved out of Ballantyne Ave and into a bigger, newer state house in the working-class suburb of Hornby. One of the first tasks Dad set himself was building a vegetable garden. He found the nearest store with hardware supplies, a giant red building called The Warehouse, and bought some seeds, a shovel and a hose. He marked out a patch of grass in the back yard, close to the hedge so as to leave plenty of room for us to play in without trampling on his seedlings.

He planted all sorts — cucumbers, tomatoes, lettuces,

spring onions, radishes, carrots. It was trial and error at first, but he has maintained a vegetable garden ever since, now extended to include raspberries and strawberries, apples, cherries and apricots.

Looking back, I can understand Dad's obsession with gardening. He had tended a plot of land for much of his life, having learnt the art of farming from his father. Amid the chaos of those early years, gardening proved to be an important outlet for Dad.

The *Tampa* parents now had a decent command of English and were employed in all sorts of fields — driving buses and taxis, working in various trades, jobs in large manufacturing firms.

After receiving his New Zealand passport, Dad was one of the first to travel back to Afghanistan in 2006. He spent some time reconnecting with old friends and family, and surveying the country he had left.

It was on this trip that he had an idea that would change our family fortunes. While transiting through Dubai, Dad met up with an old friend from the Timber Factory days. He was living in Dubai, importing car parts to sell to buyers in developing countries in the Middle East and North Africa. Dad recalled how much of a struggle it had been to sell our *saraacha* after it broke down and he couldn't get parts to fix it. Eventually we gave up and paid a scrap-metal dealer to take it off our hands.

Upon returning to Christchurch, Dad discussed with a couple of the other *Tampa* families the idea of setting up a garage that would buy old cars and salvage the working parts for export to Dubai. They would need to rent an industrial lot, get a business loan, buy trucks, forklifts and other heavy equipment, attain the appropriate licences, take on some employees, and learn about the ins and outs of running a business in New Zealand. It was a big ask.

Many of the other men balked at the idea but a few were keen. They pooled their life savings and got to work. Dad and the other men split the responsibilities evenly, from driving the tow truck to salvaging the parts to loading the containers.

From that initial conversation to filling the first container for export took them about twelve months. By late 2007, Loman Auto Parts, named after a district in Ghazni, was exporting a 40-foot container's worth of car parts every week. It helped that New Zealand has one of the oldest car fleets in the developed world.

In early 2008 Hussein began an accounting degree at Lincoln University, but at the end of the year he decided to place his studies on hold and join the business, dealing to the mass of paperwork that Dad and the others had largely ignored. This greatly helped to streamline the operation.

Two years later, Dad and Hussein sold their stake in the business and set up their own firm in Wellington. I am proud to say that Kiwi Auto Wreckers is now the largest buyer of used cars in the lower North Island and a trusted supplier of car parts. At the time of writing, our family-owned business employs more than twenty staff, with Hussein as the director, Dad having now retired.

The success of Loman Auto Parts and later Kiwi Auto Wreckers allowed us to finally move on from state housing. In 2012 we bought our own house in Christchurch, a place we could truly call our own. It was a moment of incredible pride for Mum and Dad, rivalling our citizenship ceremony. Mum had come a long way from her debilitating homesickness in those early years, and holding the keys to our own home was extra special for her.

BY THE TIME I started at Burnside High School in 2008, the first wave of *Tampa* children were heading to university. Many of the girls, including my sister Shekufah, enrolled in medical studies at the University of Otago and began to realise those childhood dreams of becoming doctors. Mum and Dad were apprehensive about their only daughter living in another city, but upon seeing the beautiful campus, they came around to the idea.

Shekufah was the first member of our family to attend university, and it was a pretty amazing accomplishment for this girl from Sungjoy. Born in a country where girls' education and female empowerment in general were shamelessly restricted, Shekufah's attaining university entrance after learning English as a teenager is a testament to her immense determination — and of course to an education system and society that supported and nurtured her ambitions.

Six years later, in 2015, she would graduate with a Master's in Microbiology. We decided this momentous occasion merited a full family road-trip to Dunedin. Shekufah was one of the first in a long line of young Afghan women who have entered Otago's prestigious medical and science programme since then.

After finishing high school, Sakhi joined the Canterbury Aero Club, where he received his pilot's licence. On his first solo flight, he flew Mum and Dad high above the Southern Alps, then along the Canterbury coastline, stopping off for a fish and chip lunch at Kaikōura. In the end Sakhi decided that being a commercial pilot would interfere too much with family life. He had married and was due to have his first child shortly. He is now the deputy director of Kiwi Auto Wreckers, and takes to the sky when the Wellington weather allows.

Ali was always the most talented athlete in the family, with a huge love of football. He was blessed with a passion and flair that few of his teammates possessed. Ali was called into the Canterbury representative football system every year during high school. He would later play for the Canterbury United Dragons in the national club competition, before accepting an athletic scholarship to California State University. Now back in New Zealand, Ali is still playing top-flight football, while also captaining the Canterbury Afghan teams in national and international football tournaments.

As for me, I finished primary and intermediate school at the top of my class, taking home the overall excellence award from the end-of-year assembly. As I began high school, Mojtaba and Mostafa were headed for Riccarton Primary School.

As at primary school, I found sports to be the best way to express myself and find mates. Athletics was one of my favourite pursuits, particularly discus. I broke the Burnside High discus record for my age group, and made it to the South Island secondary schools championships every year.

While football was my first love, a combination of ego and puberty led me to rugby. Like every Kiwi kid, I had been introduced to rugby at primary school. Having realised Ali was far more talented than I could ever be at football, I signed up to play for Burnside Rugby Club, and made the Burnside High First XV. I was the ultimate utility player, playing as a loosehead prop, centre and wing. Anyone familiar with Christchurch schoolboy rugby knows it's tough as nails, but I relished playing alongside and against my mates, some of whom, like Richie Mo'unga, would become future All Blacks.

In my last year of high school I was invited to the Canterbury representative trials. Although I didn't make the final cut, donning the red and black for the trial games was a huge moment of pride. I hope that in time, other refugee kids will do one better than me.

But my real love was books. I read anything I could get my hands on, and probably spent more time in the library than on the field. Although I loved the sciences, English was my favourite subject. In my first few weeks of high school, I noticed a poster outside the English department for the New Zealand Spelling Bee, sponsored by Vegemite. The top two from each regional final would go to the national championship in Wellington, and the national champion would earn a place at the holy grail of spelling, the Scripps National Spelling Bee in the US, as well as a year's supply of Vegemite.

I knew I stood a chance. I picked up a flyer and

registered online at the library after school. I downloaded the practice wordlist and got to work.

I took it seriously, practising for a few hours most evenings. I'd run through the thousands of words on the official list, write them down, commit them to memory while mouthing out the letters.

Acreage. Armada. Ample.

I'd silently recite lists of words while jogging around the sports field.

One of my favourite training methods was to give a dictionary to Ali, and he would flip through the pages at random and pick out a word for me to spell.

The regional spelling bee finals were held in the Riccarton High School gymnasium, the same stage I had walked across the previous year to collect my Student of the Year award. There were about 30 other word nerds there, all of us in school uniform even though it was a Saturday morning.

We were each given a numbered bib and, without any fanfare, the competition kicked off. One by one we walked up to the microphone, listened for our word and then spelled it out.

Orchestra. Oxymoronic. Orthopaedic.

With a few parents and siblings in the audience watching in silence, the 30 vocabulary enthusiasts were eliminated one by one. Soon enough it was just me, a girl, and 28 empty chairs on stage.

We went back and forth, neck and neck, and eventually exhausted the prepared wordlist. We took a brief break during which officials hunted down a secondary list. While the girl chatted with her family, I looked around the room, as I had no one there that day.

The competition resumed and we went back to trading blows like heavyweight boxers.

Until soliloquy.

S-O-L-I-L-O-Q-U-E-Y.

The warm ding of the bell that I had heard in response to my answers all afternoon was replaced by a cold buzzer.

Rookie mistake. Of course I knew that not all Q-Us are followed by another vowel.

I came second, but at least I had secured a spot in the national finals. We were each handed a basket of prizes, including vouchers, a 1700-page *Oxford Dictionary* (the irony was not lost on me), tickets to Wellington – and jars of Vegemite.

The national finals rolled around quickly. I continued training, perusing the *Oxford Dictionary* to find words I didn't know how to spell. My mind soaked up new words like a sponge.

I was allowed to take a family member, so Hussein and

I flew to Wellington a day before the championship. It was a first for both of us. We took in the beautiful Wellington coastline on our descent and wondered briefly, along with most people flying into the capital for the first time, whether the pilot was going to crash into the rocky harbour.

Competition day was a gloomy wet Sunday. I could make out Hussein's face in the back, just beyond the blinding spotlights. We began, and a rapid pace was soon set. No one fell in the first few rounds, as they had in our regional competition. I knew this was going to be a tight race. Morning turned into afternoon. With the rain pounding on the roof and with attention spans faltering, the word warriors began to fall, until it was just myself and two others left.

Then came silhouetted.

S-I-L-H-O-U-E-T-E-D.

The buzzer deflated me like an air mattress. Another rookie mistake. How could I forget the double consonant following an O-U-E?

I was now officially the third-best speller in New Zealand. The other two continued for a few more rounds, during which I sat in the back next to Hussein. He said he was proud of me. I was pretty proud of me too.

There was more Vegemite all round. To this day it tastes of bitter defeat.

I received a shiny bronze medal with the words Spelling Bee imprinted on it, as well as a small cash prize. A couple of local journalists were milling around and one of them, noticing my name, asked where I was from. I told him I was from Afghanistan and we had arrived on the *Tampa*.

I thought no more about it, but the next day my brother's cellphone was going off with calls from reporters all across the country. They all wanted to speak to the refugee kid who had won the spelling bee. I told them I came third; they should interview the kid who won. But they were far more interested in the young refugee who had learnt his alphabet at the Mangere Refugee Resettlement Centre.

A few days later, back in Christchurch, a reporter came to our house. She snapped a horrible photo of me sitting on our Afghan carpet, dictionary in lap, one arm in a bright green cast (I had broken it some weeks earlier being unathletic), a chubby face and a bowl cut. That photo haunts me to this day. It was in the school newsletter and in the papers I was distributing on my paper runs. I couldn't get away from it and it felt like my privacy had been breached.

My parents, however, were extremely proud. They were stunned when the news eventually made its way to Afghanistan — my uncle there called to say they had recognised my face in their local daily! It was the first time they had seen me since we'd left seven years earlier. They felt a weird mix of emotions — I'm sure there's a word to describe it . . .

SOME WEEKS LATER, at the Homework Club, a representative of Te Papa Tongarewa, the national museum in Wellington, told us of an upcoming exhibition dedicated to the refugee experience in New Zealand. They were seeking participants. Being self-conscious teenagers, none of us was about to volunteer.

'Abbas would be great! He won the national spelling bee!' yelled Ali.

'I only came third,' I corrected him irritably.

'That's great! Bronze is just aged gold,' said the curator.

The next weekend about twenty teenagers from refugee families gathered for a full-day workshop. We produced poetry, videos and photos reflecting the lives of refugees. We were invited to the opening of the exhibition in 2009; this was my second trip to the capital in as many years. I proudly watched as our world was unveiled to the audience. At the time of writing, the 'Mixing Room' exhibition was still on display at Te Papa.

ABOVE Backpacking through Myanmar in 2015 was an eye-opening experience.

LEFT With some of the children in Sungjoy on my second visit in 2017.

ABOVE LEFT Doorway to our homestead in Sungjoy. I took this photo on my first trip back to Afghanistan in 2012.

ABOVE RIGHT At a market in Mazar-e-Sharif. Afghanistan has so much to offer.

BELOW Sunset over Sungjoy.

ABOVE Dad and me in Sungjoy on my first visit back in 2012.

BELOW Ali, Dad and me helping a Sungjoy family with their apricot harvest in 2017.

OPPOSITE ABOVE My semester abroad in Singapore was a period of immense personal growth.

OPPOSITE BELOW Graduating from the University of Canterbury was one of the happiest days of my life. This is what Mum and Dad had dreamed of.

RIGHT Mum and Dad have seen and sacrificed so much. Seeing them finally at peace is the ultimate prize.

BELOW Mum and Dad with twin grandsons Kam and Nik, Sakhi's second and third kids.

LEFT Spinning yarns at a berry farm with my nieces Nazanin and Mohanna. 'Your uncle had the record for the most berries picked in a day.'

BELOW The outdoors were a fantastic way to get some headspace during the university years. My best mate, Naz, took this photo of me hiking up Temple Basin, Southern Alps.

OPPOSITE ABOVE How good is New Zealand?

OPPOSITE BELOW Talking to New Zealand with Mike McRoberts one week after 15 March.

ABOVE LEFT Making memories with Genevieve in the US.

ABOVE RIGHT A few weeks after this photo was taken, history would test Washington with a global pandemic, massive civil unrest, and political turmoil.

LEFT Graduating from Georgetown. We've come a long way from the ESOL class at Riccarton Primary School. I consider myself incredibly fortunate to be on this journey.

ON 22 FEBRUARY 2011, I was in the library at Burnside High when the walls began to rattle and the floor moved under our feet. It was another enormous earthquake, this one 6.3 on the Richter scale. I immediately checked in with my parents, and within an hour we were all home. We were lucky that Hornby, being in the more stable western suburbs, was largely unscathed. But in the eastern suburbs and central city the damage was devastating, and 185 people lost their lives.

The quake six months earlier had been bigger — 7.1 — but no one had been killed. Now the city that we had explored almost every weekend was unrecognisable, and was suddenly the centre of national and international attention. Words such as munted, liquefaction and resilience became synonymous with Christchurch.

But the earthquakes had one upside for the Afghan refugee community. Many had completed trades training by then — tiling, plumbing and all manner of other hands-on craftsmanship — enabling families to build up a substantial financial base. Small mum-and-dad tiling operations sprang up just in time to reap the windfall of the earthquake rebuild.

Other Afghan-owned businesses were also popping up across Christchurch, starting with a halal butchery and soon including two Afghan restaurants, a Middle Eastern supermarket, a bakery and a tailoring service. Within a decade of arriving in New Zealand, many *Tampa* families owned their own homes and businesses. In recent years, *Tampa* family members have ventured into property development, the professional services and academia.

In 2011 some of this new-found wealth went to a communal fund to purchase a community centre. After a decade of renting spaces for their events, the United Afghan Association of Canterbury bought a community hall in the suburb of Bishopdale. This would be the venue for all future events — religious, cultural, celebratory or commemorative. It remains the hub of all community events today.

Through determined entrepreneurialism and hard work, the *Tampa* families were beginning to realise the Kiwi dream.

As we started finding our place in society, our community's civic engagement began to grow. In the initial years it had been pretty low; everyone was fully occupied with the basics, such as housing and language and just getting by. But as the years went by, people began to take an interest in politics. As the 2005 general election approached, many of the newly minted Kiwis and first-time voters were less interested in political policy than in showing their gratitude to the politician who had rescued them from the Pacific. This meant there was solid support for the Labour Party and Prime Minister Helen Clark.

By the time the next generation reached voting age, their civic and political engagement had increased significantly. Although my parents' generation remained dyed-in-the-wool Labour Party supporters, the younger generation have a variety of political leanings. Many Afghan families made significant progress under the National government led by Prime Minister John Key. (The fact that he had also attended Burnside High was a bonus.) With the economy booming and billions being poured into the Christchurch rebuild, many saw their livelihoods skyrocket. Like all Kiwis, they tended to support the political party they felt best represented their interests. Regardless of political affiliations, there is a deep sense of gratitude among our community to Aotearoa New Zealand. The progress made thus far is a testament to the people and policies that have nurtured our desire to better ourselves.

AS WELL AS success, we all experienced moments of 'learning', shall we say. It would be a gross oversight if I didn't mention that some of us had a few brushes with the law along the way. Many were driving-related, and some others resulted from being unaware of the rules. But a few involved simply breaking the law and being caught, and having to own our mistakes.

One day, after a community barbecue for Nowruz, the Afghan New Year, a group of us teens decided to go for a swim. The nearest place was the upscale neighbourhood of Pegasus Town, with a bridge spanning an artificial lake at the centre of the manicured rows of houses. We ignored the sign and decided to jump off the bridge into the cool waters below, spending the better part of the afternoon there. As we were packing up to leave, we saw two police cars speeding towards us, lights ablaze. They were responding to a report of 'two carloads of large males acting recklessly'. The officers questioned us, and we all had a good laugh, then went home.

I thought that was the end of it, but two weeks later a private security contractor came knocking to deliver a trespass notice.

Mum, busy sewing in the lounge, asked who was at the door.

I pocketed the piece of paper and said it was some kids selling chocolate for a school fundraiser. Mum was none the wiser.

Another time, a group of us were caught shoplifting from a mall and held by police until Mum came to pick us up. I feared the worst.

'Abbas, I'm not angry,' she said. 'I'm disappointed.'

To any child, disappointing Mum is one of the worst things. It was a silent car ride home.

But perhaps the biggest learning moment was during a barbecue to mark the end of Ramadan in May. More than a hundred families drove out to a lovely spot in the country. As the adults set out the blankets and got the grill ready, we kids wandered off to explore. We came across a dairy. With food a couple of hours off, and no money in our pockets, and simply because we were a group of young boys, we thought it would be a great idea to steal an entire two-litre tub of ice cream.

With the subtlety of an All Blacks haka, one boy tucked the tub into his jersey while the rest of us acted nonchalant and tried to distract the shopkeeper.

We scarpered out the door and found a shady spot to wolf down the spoils.

Later that day, as we all gathered for a meal of steaming naan and grilled kebabs, a police car pulled up.

Everyone looked mystified.

Had we booked the wrong date for the venue?

Were we making too much noise?

None of the above. A police officer called out that they wanted to speak with 'the boys who have indulged in some cookies and crime'.

My co-offenders and I looked at one another, willing a

hole in the ground to open up and swallow us all, but the earth remained firm.

With our parents looking completely confused, naan-wrapped kebabs in hand, I eventually got to my feet.

'Yes, I can help you with that,' I said.

There were gasps from all around. Abbas, the spelling bee golden boy, was a wanted criminal!

I walked towards the police officer, feeling the piercing gaze of every eyeball around me. The silence was palpable.

Then my uncle, bless him, defused the tension by saying to me, 'Thank you, Abbas, for being a young leader for us. Please assist this gentleman in finding the suspects.'

Cool as ice, my uncle had saved the day and ended my embarrassment. Everyone went back to the food and festivities, grateful to have the police leave, and one of their own assisting them in their enquiries.

Out of sight of the community, I faced the dairy owner with the police standing beside me, arms crossed. I accepted full responsibility and apologised. I didn't nark on the others, but they all signed the apology letter I drafted.

That encounter — and others since — reinforced one of the central tenets of Afghan and indeed many other communities, particularly Asian communities. It is that I am one piece of a much larger puzzle. My successes reflect on my family and community, as do my failures. Just as my successes are a point of pride for the community, my failures can be a blight on the entire village.

I am grateful that we had these learning opportunities, as those are the moments of greatest growth. It has been a lesson that I have applied in many aspects of my day-to-day life, and has been a touchstone when I am facing any major decision in life.

20.
THERE AND
BACK AGAIN

Tūrangawaewae – a place of belonging.

Watan – homeland.

BOTH THESE WORDS describe the place where you can trace your roots deep into the earth. Understandably, a lot of displaced families struggle with finding theirs. Many have fled conflict and persecution of an ethnic or tribal nature, so their homeland is disputed.

While children by and large are agile in pursuing their identity and adapting their connections to a home, adults can really struggle, torn between the old home and the new.

Adjusting to living in a foreign country and an

entirely different culture is immensely difficult for adults in particular. It's not just the physical barriers, such as language or customs; there's a huge mental shift also. I know of one family whose parents decided to move back to Afghanistan after gaining their New Zealand citizenship. Well-respected members of their community in Kabul, they just couldn't cope in Christchurch. Then, less than a year after moving back, they returned to New Zealand, having realised the challenges of adjustment in a foreign land were nothing compared with the dangers they faced every day back home.

Some elderly parents and relatives decline the offer of family reunification visas, choosing to spend their remaining years in the land they have always known. And many immigrants choose a middle way and travel back and forth between the two.

Mum and Dad have been back to Afghanistan a number of times, as have other *Tampa* parents. Given the distance, and the numerous friends and family members to be visited, these trips are often months long.

In the early years I questioned these trips, asking why they would choose to spend months travelling to an impoverished and conflict-ridden part of the world. But I understood when I went back to Afghanistan for the first time — in 2012, aged eighteen.

Flying into Kabul, the first thing I noticed was the mountains. Seeing them from above, they were not unlike the mountains of the Southern Alps. Jagged peaks rising formidably into the heavens, sliced by crystal-clear rivers and surrounded by lush fertile plains.

I was nervous as I walked through passport control at Hamid Karzai International Airport — named after the country's first president. My pre-season rugby training meant I was bigger than most of the other men in line. The gel in my hair made me stand out even further as it gleamed in the sun and caught dust easily. Even though this was the country of my birth, I felt like a foreigner in my Chuck Taylors, my black jeans and my H&M jacket. I took note of the *peran tumban* and waistcoat combo that appeared to be the fashion among the local males my age. I couldn't help but notice the looks I was receiving from those around me. They seemed to be wondering who I was but were hesitant to ask.

The passport control officer took a second glance at my passport and then back at me. I could understand his dilemma. I stood before him partially resembling an Afghan, with a New Zealand passport that looked a little too fancy for his liking.

'Welcome home, brother,' he said eventually, as he stamped my passport.

I felt tears welling in my eyes at the word 'home'.

My return to Afghanistan hadn't been planned. I was in Athens at the end of a month-long trip through Greece and Italy as part of Burnside High's classical studies curriculum.

I vividly remember the phone call from my uncle in Kabul.

'Salaam, is that Abbas?'

'Yes, *Kakay*, it's me. How are you?'

'Great! Since you're only a few hours by plane away from your homeland you should stop by.'

There was a profound silence at this point as I contemplated what to say.

'I hear your classics tour was meant to be educational; well, I can guarantee that you will learn more about the world from a day in Kabul than from all your textbooks.'

I knew he was right. I had always wanted to go back — but not like this. I wasn't prepared. But when else would I have the chance? I wondered. And my Dad was there . . .

The next thing I knew, it was all arranged.

My uncle would pick me up from the airport, and Dad would join us a few days later from Mazar-e-Sharif. I called Mum once I had booked my flight. I could sense her anxiety as she offered advice. Avoid eye contact with strangers. Don't ask the soldiers for photos. Don't ask *anyone* for photos. And so on. The thought of her boy making the trip back home was clearly nerve-racking, but there was a hint of pride. Perhaps deep down, she knew this was destined to happen.

Uncle Ali spotted me wandering aimlessly at the civilian pick-up point, which was inconveniently located as far as possible from the terminals. The last time I had seen this man I was seven and I was afraid I wouldn't recognise him. Thankfully, he recognised me. I have inherited my father's facial structure and this, along with the fact that I clearly had no idea what I was doing, assured him that I was the one.

'What are they feeding you down there?' he asked as he gave me a hug and the customary three kisses on the cheek.

We drove through the numerous checkpoints out of the airport and eventually entered Kabul. I had never been there before so I had no idea what to expect – except from what I had seen on television. It's impossible to describe a city like Kabul. You can travel all over the world and you'll not find a city quite like it. It seemed like a mixing bowl of every type of person the world had to offer. It was a city trying to find itself. Time had apparently got mixed up in Kabul, and the past and the future seemed to be competing to make the present.

Following lunch, we drove through the thriving new

suburb of Hajji Nabi, where expensive villas were under construction and apartments were being built into the hillsides. We walked the grounds of the ruins of the Darul Aman Palace. In its prime, it would have rivalled the manors and country estates of the European aristocrats, but now it bore the scars of decades of conflict, with mortar and bullet wounds rendering most of it a heap of rubble. But like the Christchurch Cathedral after the earthquakes, it still had an air of glory about it.

Dad joined us the next day and we explored the rest of Kabul, taking in the ancient bazaars and vibrant street scenes, and even picnicking on the banks of Qargha Lake, a beautiful azure-coloured reservoir that rivals Lake Tekapo.

The next day we would head for Sungjoy. I felt incredibly nervous.

We left Kabul before dawn, and after eight hours on a dirt road I was back in my village. It was the most extraordinary feeling to walk through the valleys and climb the hills that were my childhood home. All those memories flooded back. It was almost an out-of-body experience.

Our house was still in good shape. My uncle would live there when he needed an escape from Kabul, but otherwise it was looked after by a nomadic family. They tended to the gardens in exchange for free accommodation.

A few of my cousins and former classmates turned

out to welcome Dad and me. Clearly, my uncle had given them a heads-up, as they had a feast of freshly baked naan and biryani ready and waiting. Before long, the exhausting road-trip coupled with the emotional rollercoaster of my return hit me like a freight train, and I fell into a deep sleep under the thatched roof of a house I had not lived in for over a decade.

THE NEXT DAY we visited my aunty, who lived in a little homestead a few hours' drive from Sungjoy. She had apparently been there at my birth, but I had no memory of her from my childhood. I wondered if she would recognise me after all these years. Just over a mountain pass, we came to an idyllic stream surrounded by tall conifers. I was driving my uncle's Toyota Surf, and the potholed dirt road reminded me of the gravel roads of the Canterbury backcountry.

We hiked up a hillside until we came to a house perched in a clearing. It was like walking into the cover of a *National Geographic* magazine. The house was an historical relic — it could have sat happily alongside the whare at the national museum. It was short and stout, with low doors, simple clay walls and one crooked window with a faded blue frame. The roof was made of straw held together with clay, and the timber supports jutted out unevenly. Exposed logs created a veranda on one side, providing shelter for a neat stack of firewood and an assortment of tools and household items — a large metal bucket, an axe, a roll of tarpaulin, some plastic jerry cans, a clay pot. A stack of fabric stained with apricot and mulberry juices.

The door swung open and a short, feisty-looking woman ran out with the determination of Jonah Lomu. She wore a once-colourful dress, the everyday variety that many Afghan women wear around the house; hers was a faded olive, having perhaps started out as a vibrant blue. Over the top she wore a more colourful vest, embroidered with a gold band and bejewelled with shiny pieces of metal and glass.

'Abbas *jaan*! Where have you been all my life? You were just a child when you left — look at you now! You have a beard! I used to hold you up against my chest when you were crying, and now look how grown up you are!'

I kissed her calloused hands; rough, brown hands that had seen a lifetime of toil.

'It's good to see you, *Khalay*.'

Tears started rolling down her wrinkled face.

'You can still speak your mother tongue! I thought you might have forgotten where you come from. Hajji, is this one married yet?' she asked, finally acknowledging Dad, addressing him by his title rather than his name. Formality still rules, even between siblings.

'No, but maybe you have someone in mind?'

We all laughed and she invited us inside.

Walking into her house was like travelling back in time. The entranceway split in two. To the right and two steps down was the *qoto*, a small manger underneath the house, similar to a garage or basement. I spotted two cows, a donkey, some goats and half a dozen chickens. It smelled like animals, but I loved that they looked comfortable. If Mary had arrived carrying Jesus that day, she would have found a bed that rivalled any in Bethlehem.

To the left and two steps up was the entrance to the lounge.

We sat on the floor, propped against the walls with some comfortable pillows. On one wall hung an ancient long gun, like a colonial-era musket.

Noticing my interest in it, Aunty said it had belonged to her granddad. He used it to hunt rabbits and wolves, and scare off any intruders, but it had not fired a bullet in decades.

A young woman appeared with a tray of tea in glass cups and colourful sweets. Two young boys clung to her dress like little bear cubs. Aunty had one son, a few years older than me, who was currently in a refugee camp in Turkey, waiting to cross into Greece and beyond. He had left his wife and two boys with his mother while he went in search of a better life for them all.

The boys, aged five and three, could scarcely remember their father, who had left more than a year ago. They were curious about Dad and me; clearly they didn't have many visitors. If I had known there would be children, I would have brought gifts. Dad dug into his pockets and took out a handful of lollies and passed them to me. I opened my hands to show them, and they took the bait. We were best friends from then on.

I listened as Aunty spoke of how the winters were no longer predictable. At 60 years old she was a hardy woman, and I could picture her at home in New Zealand in a pair of Red Bands and a Swanndri. She spoke of the ongoing struggle to get food and medicine. The issue was not money but accessibility. Now that her son, the sole breadwinner, was gone, most of the heavy lifting fell to her. Her daughter-in-law had slipped on some ice the previous winter and was still nursing a broken arm in a flimsy fabric cast.

The boys would soon reach school age and would have to walk an hour each way. They would need sturdy shoes and school supplies. The village networks that had sustained people throughout the most difficult times no longer existed. In times of relative stability, villagers had been materially poorer but had enjoyed immense richness in their community support networks, which gave them strength to weather the storms. The exodus of families, beginning with the Soviet invasion and accelerating in the 1990s, meant those networks were broken.

Aunty was proud of her younger brother for taking the risk of packing up his family and leaving in search of safer harbours. She knew she had missed that boat. I felt tears well up as she spoke of her loneliness and her concern for her grandsons, who would be fatherless for God knew how long.

I needed some fresh air and made for the door. Forgetting how low it was, I managed to hit the top of the frame squarely with my nose.

The boys were glued to my side and insisted on showing me around, pointing out rocks that lizards sunned themselves on, the biggest ant nests and their favourite mulberry tree.

As we bid goodbye, Dad handed his sister some US banknotes, as well as a length of fabric that Mum had picked out for her. She cried and asked when I would be back. I said I didn't know but that I would look into getting her New Zealand residency. We both knew it was an empty promise. She would never leave.

I wondered how Dad felt about leaving her; I asked

him as we walked back to the car. It was clear that her situation was worrying him but he knew there was nothing he could do. She was a fiercely independent woman who would make her own way.

On the way back, we stopped by what I thought was an abandoned *masjid*. It had a faded blue dome, and the front door was crooked and barely attached to its rusted hinges. The main window was boarded up, but as we got closer, a man emerged from around the back. He wore a dark robe and had a long mane of dark, greasy hair. He beckoned for us to follow him into the abandoned shed by way of a back door.

It turned out he was a fortune-teller, a shaman and witchdoctor all rolled into one. As Dad talked to him, I felt like Harry Potter observing Professor Snape in a potions class. Although Islam is the official religion of Afghanistan, mysticism and ancient rituals play a significant role in the lives of many. People like this man blend religious scripture, mysticism and fortune-telling into a heady mix for the gullible, boldly proclaiming one's prospects in matters such as marriage, business, family feuds, exams and the next season's harvest.

Dad asked him for a simple traveller's prayer to keep me safe on the many journeys I would take through life. The shaman took my palm, gazed at it like Saruman peering into the Palantir, and mouthed some incantations in a language I didn't understand. After a few minutes he released my hand, opened his eyes and began scribbling letters I couldn't read. His hand moved across the page frenetically, penning characters that looked like runes and hieroglyphs. Then he folded the paper into a neat triangle and wrapped it in a piece of purple fabric, which he proceeded to sew shut. He placed the token in my hand and closed my fingers over it.

'It is written; it must not be read.' These were his first and only words to me throughout the whole encounter.

My mind flashed to *The Alchemist* by Paulo Coelho, one of my favourite books.

I am not particularly religious or superstitious, and nor do I believe a roadside practitioner wields influence in my life, but I still have the purple pouch, unopened.

IN NEW ZEALAND, Dad is a reserved and introverted man, quietly going about his day, attending English-language classes, gardening, working around the house. Although he is proud of the risks he's taken to get us to where we are today, he still has some questions. He wishes we'd come to New Zealand some twenty years earlier than we did, when he was younger and could really have made the most of the opportunity. I sense a 'What if?' that lingers in the minds of many older refugees, who see their kids outpacing them in their new homelands.

But in Afghanistan, I saw a confident man in his element. Pockets flush with cash, a wide network of friends, and the respect and recognition he spent a lifetime building. Several times, sitting down for a cup of tea with his friends, I'd hear stories about Dad I'd never heard before — of a lifetime of struggles and victories that occurred before my time. Children become obsessed with their own growth and ambitions, forgetting that their parents were also once children who grew up and built lives. This is so for all children of all parents, but for refugee parents, the past is sometimes buried very deep.

Adult refugees find the transition to a new life incredibly hard. An invisible battle rages internally between the old ways and the new, soothed by return visits and online chats.

For our part, we children grew used to our parents being either half or fully absent from time to time. Ali and I would be playing football or rugby, and while the sidelines would be packed with parents and supporters, our mum and dad were usually absent. Football and rugby were played in the New Zealand winter, meaning it was early summer in Afghanistan, the ideal time to visit. We drove ourselves to the games or hitched a ride with other parents. When asked, we'd say our parents were working or busy with community matters. We signed our own school permission slips and paid any fees due or tried our best to avoid them. Sometimes I resented the situation I was in.

A psychologist might diagnose us with parental deficit disorder, but we just accepted it as the norm. It wasn't just the physical distance. We children had raced ahead in adapting to our new surroundings. Mum and Dad were by then capable and confident enough to drive to the supermarket, attend classes, talk to neighbours and even answer the phone. But we had grown up in New Zealand, and saw the world through a lens they couldn't.

By the time my siblings and I were teenagers, the gulf between our parents and ourselves had widened into the Grand Canyon. New Zealand was our tūrangawaewae, our *watan*. At times their perspective was so at odds with ours it was like we were from different planets. While we had our feet firmly set, they were still in search of their *watan*. Where we had grounded ourselves totally in New Zealand and a new way of life, they were floating between two worlds. After overcoming so many challenges, one of the remaining obstacles — one of the hardest issues to resolve for refugees — is the puzzle of identity.

While I fully support refugee services, they cannot fix

everything. The question of identity and belonging cannot be settled by some government policy.

We were lucky because the *Tampa* families were jointly resettled in Christchurch and could lean on one another for support. As the community has grown, newer arrivals have an established community network to tap into. The Farsi school, Homework Club, sports tournaments, Eid festivals and community barbecues are such examples.

There are countless examples of community building that I can recall. In the early years, a relative of a community member, living in Kabul, needed emergency surgery to remove a malignant tumour. Within days Afghan families had raised the funds needed. Another time, when a dozen-strong group of Christchurch Afghans completed their Hajj pilgrimage, the entire community welcomed them back with a communal feast to mark the rite of passage.

Such initiatives provide a strong sense of belonging that eventually helps to close the chasm. But sadly, such communities can wither and disappear as the second and third generations feel less need for them. Research suggests that it is the transition from the first to the second generation that is most crucial for the community to thrive. If the first generation established the foundations, then it is up to the second generation to build the house, and for future generations to fill and maintain the house.

While I grumbled about my parents' return visits to Afghanistan for their effect on me, after my own trip in 2012 I came to understand their predicament. I sympathised.

I am glad to report that over the last decade, as their children have blossomed and continued to put down roots, Mum and Dad are increasingly at ease about their place in New Zealand. Home is where the heart is, and for Mum and Dad, their hearts are wherever their children are happiest.

21.

THE

UNIVERSITY

YEARS

SOME WEEKS AFTER returning from Afghanistan in 2012, I caught up with former Christchurch mayor Garry Moore. We talked at length about my trip and how I felt I had a new appreciation of my parents, and a renewed sense of myself. Garry suggested I talk at the upcoming Christchurch TEDx convention. Seeing the puzzled look on my face, he showed me some talks from the 2011 convention, which had largely focused on the Canterbury rebuild.

'The idea is simple: you get on stage and just share your story. I think yours will really resonate with Kiwis, not to mention those Aussies,' he said.

I said I'd consider it. I enjoyed public speaking but

wanted to make sure my family were comfortable with me sharing our story so publicly. After a conversation with them over dinner I agreed to speak at the convention. With the earthquakes having seriously damaged most of Christchurch's larger venues, that year's convention was held in the Burnside High School auditorium — familiar ground for me!

The speakers seemed to be focused again on the rebuild, and the opportunity to reimagine Christchurch from the ground up and build a vibrant new city. Engineers, volunteers, community organisers and business advocates spoke of a city that would be stronger, more evolved, while retaining its familiar charm.

When it came time for me to speak, I felt like the odd one out. What did I have to contribute to this discussion? Everyone else's ideas I could envisage woven together into a beautiful cloak. I blanked. I stuttered and stumbled, completely ignored my prepared script, the blaring red countdown numbers on the timer. I made a joke about exactly that and the audience laughed, which put me at ease.

Then I regathered myself and began telling the story of how I came to be standing on that stage. The audience was silent throughout my talk and I could not make out any faces among the bright lights. The next thing I knew, my time was up and the light was flashing to tell me to stop.

I looked out into the silent darkness and the audience erupted into a standing ovation. I was very chuffed.

Afterwards, people came up and thanked me for sharing my story. Their reaction made me realise how little people actually knew about refugees and the refugee crisis. They might have seen some statistics, or read the odd article, but they had little understanding of the horrors that drove people to leave their homes, the hardships along the way, or how much a fresh start can mean.

LIKE MANY LEAVING high school, I didn't really know what I wanted to do with my life. I considered joining the family business, perhaps as a truck driver, or handling the paperwork with Hussein. The Canterbury rebuild was also in full swing by now, and I considered going into the trades. Some of my mates had recently moved to Western Australia, where they had been lured by highpaying jobs in the booming mining sector, and I considered joining them.

I briefly considered joining the military. I had watched a New Zealand Defence Force display of military hardware, including a mock firefight, and it had got me thinking. The venue was next to an aged-care facility, and I watched as dozens of veterans, rows of badges pinned to their chests, were shown around the display in their wheelchairs and chatted with their younger comrades in arms. Some mounted armoured personnel carriers and sat behind large guns, undoubtedly reliving the glory days.

I talked to one veteran who had served in Korea and Vietnam. He recalled how the incessant tropical heat gave them painful skin lesions that were exacerbated by their heavy cotton uniforms. But what he mostly remembered was the brotherhood and camaraderie that held the men together during these challenging times. Willie Apiata had recently been awarded the Victoria Cross, and his dogged determination and bravery in a firefight against the Taliban was front-page news.

I made some enquiries, and was directed to the cadet programmes. Out of all the branches of the armed forces, the air force felt like the best fit. I imagined flying over distant lands, looking down at people and places as I had on my first ever plane ride. So I joined the No. 18 (Avon) Squadron of the Air Training Corps, the cadet programme for the Royal New Zealand Air Force (RNZAF). We would meet in the evenings once a week at the decommissioned Wigram Air Force Base. As with all things military, it was a highly regimented scheme. We would arrive in uniform, a toned-down yet smart version of the official RZNAF dress uniform. Our Number 1s, as we called this getup, consisted of black dress shoes polished to the highest sheen, navy trousers with crisp creases, black belt and light blue collared shirt, dressed with an official name badge, any earned insignia, and a triangular cap.

We would assemble for inspection by the staff sergeant.

'Nazari, give those shoes a better shine — I want to see my reflection.'

We would start with drills where we marched in formation. Then there were lessons on military history, aerodynamics, navigation, outdoor survival and physical and mental health. We learnt to read topographical maps, and how to safely navigate difficult terrain.

I loved the structure and discipline, and the focus on holding oneself to a high standard.

Once a month we would spend a weekend practising our navigation and teamwork skills. One weekend exercise at Burnham Military Camp we spent the day learning marksmanship and first aid. Come nightfall, we employed our terrain navigation and covert tactics in a giant game of Capture the Flag. We were soldiers behind enemy lines.

The highlight of the year was the Anzac Day dawn service. Every cadet from all the armed services would assemble a few blocks from the Christchurch Cathedral. We would march in formation, behind veterans and active service men and women, all in our Number 1s. We would stand at attention for parts of the service, and those who had not obeyed the order to eat breakfast swayed like trees in the wind.

I loved the sound of the bugle, and the bagpipes. Kiwi culture doesn't have much pomp and ceremony, but we laid it all out there on Anzac Day.

Mum and Dad didn't fully understand my interest in the military, but they dropped me off and picked me up when I needed them to. Mum was particularly enamoured with my uniform, incessantly taking photos to share with her sisters back in Afghanistan. But after a couple of years of cadetship, I concluded that my heart wasn't in it. While I appreciated the skills I had learnt, I realised I was mainly thrill-seeking, which is never a good reason to do anything.

ON THE LAST day of high school, when I was signing off my textbooks, one of the office staff handed me a letter they had found as they were clearing the reception desk. The envelope had my name on it and no one knew how long it had sat there unnoticed.

I tore open the envelope. It was a letter from someone who had been at my TEDx talk. They were a student at Harvard University and reckoned I would have a shot of getting in as well. I read the letter over and over again in disbelief. Here I am on the very last day of school, and a letter arrives out of the blue to guide me on the next step of my journey. I showed the letter to a few friends, and they reckoned it was surely a sign from above.

I had not considered attending an American college, but now I couldn't get the thought out of my head. A few friends I spoke to all thought I had a decent shot as well. It was too late for the next intake, but surely worth applying the following year. I had already accepted a scholarship to the University of Canterbury, but promised myself I would revisit this possibility further down the road.

Meanwhile, I enrolled in a law degree at Canterbury. I needed some paying work as well, and I had heard of real estate agents making eye-watering money in the booming post-quake market. So the summer before lectures started, I walked into a real estate office close to campus and they immediately offered me an apprentice position. I was to attend staff meetings and shadow two of their top agents while studying towards my licence.

My weekends consisted of preparing and attending open homes and auctions and learning other aspects of the trade. I spent most mornings calling people who had attended the weekend's open homes. I walked into university lectures wearing a button-down shirt and often a tie, distinctly at odds with the usual uniform of hoody and shorts.

I hobbled through the rest of the year balancing this work with law school, but eventually it dawned on me that I was enjoying neither of them. While I enjoyed meeting and talking to different people at open homes, I had no drive to clinch real estate deals. And law school was dry and boring — like eating Weet-Bix without milk.

The following summer holiday I signed up to Student Job Search and took on a huge variety of jobs. I worked at a fruit and vegetable cold-storage facility, sorted mail at a courier warehouse, poured a concrete driveway, helped a dozen families move into their permanent post-earthquake home, packed 40-foot containers full of ornate wooden furniture, put up a retaining wall, and replaced earthquake-damaged sewerage and stormwater pipes.

One of my favourite jobs was weeding a large lifestyle block in Tai Tapu. When I got there a lovely gentleman greeted me with a calloused handshake. He had been a farmer his entire life and planned to build his dream home on the hillside facing the Southern Alps. The job was advertised as a full week's work, given the property's acreage and hilly terrain.

Feeling fit and confident, I asked for a wager — if I finished the work in less than the advertised 40 hours, I would be paid for the full week as advertised. We shook hands and I got to work. He showed me how to mix the weedkiller at the right ratio, and how to use the hoe to pull out larger weeds. I strapped the fifteen-litre weed-sprayer to my back and off I went, starting from the top corner and working my way down methodically. Once the sprayer was empty, I would pull out a couple of the tree-sized weeds, hoist them over my shoulder and walk them down to a pile by the barn, refill the sprayer and repeat.

I did this for three days, arriving at dawn with a packed lunch and working until late afternoon. Like berry-picking, it was demanding work, but I found immense satisfaction in seeing the hillside tamed by my hands. The farmer was chuffed that I had finished early and handed me $1200 in crisp $50 notes — more than what I earned for a month's worth of open homes.

At the start of my second year I swapped from law to history and political science. I also put my real estate licence on hold, promising them I'd be back after my studies finished. So far that hasn't happened . . .

I consulted some of my friends about my decision to change degrees, including Naz, one of my best childhood mates. This straight-talking engineering student was unimpressed.

'What are you going to do with that degree? Are you going to go work at the history factory? Or maybe the new political science plant that's just opened down the road. At least with law, you can be a lawyer.'

I laughed it off. I wasn't too bothered about job prospects. I knew that if I focused on studies I found enjoyable and worked hard, the rest of it would work itself out.

I STARTED TO enjoy my studies. Attending lectures, reading for hours in the library – like in my spelling bee days, I soaked it all up like a sponge. I strongly believe this is what university should be – an opportunity to expand one's knowledge and horizons away from the pressures and distractions of 'real life'.

Not playing any sport that year freed up my weekends and I found an appreciation for the outdoors. It started with a volunteering project for a local Rotary club. The Student Volunteer Army, a youth-run volunteer organisation established to help with the cleanup after the earthquakes, encouraged students to tackle a volunteering project every semester. I signed up for some track regeneration work in the hills around Christchurch.

One hot April weekend we trudged up the hillside overlooking Diamond Harbour, hauling spades, shovels and wheelbarrows. Heavy rainfall had left the track in bad shape. Our team of student volunteers got to work to re-form the track, cutting into the muddy earth and barrowing it to other areas that needed it. We cut drainage channels, removed debris, and lopped fallen branches and hedges. It was sweaty, tiring work, but seeing the end result was rewarding. Over lunch, one of the Rotarians told us how his view of our generation had changed. He had believed young people were selfish, soft and scared to get their hands dirty, but the work of the Student Volunteer Army had made him realise we weren't a bad lot.

HAVING ENJOYED THE previous summer so much, and learnt so many skills, I planned to follow the same game plan the following summer. Soon after my last exam, I reactivated my Student Job Search account and set about picking the jobs that sounded most demanding and the best paid. I had only completed one job, pouring concrete foundations for a garage, when I received an email that would change everything.

A few months earlier, I had applied for a place on a university trip to Southeast Asia, and the email confirmed my place. Six weeks of intensive coursework at Victoria University of Wellington would be followed by a six-week field study across seven countries in Southeast Asia, observing New Zealand's role in the region. I was stoked!

I moved to Wellington for the pre-departure coursework, staying with Hussein and his wife, Sharifah, who was also studying at Victoria. Hussein was happy to have another pair of hands at the Kiwi Auto Wreckers yard during the summer rush. I would wake up before dawn and open the yard, work until midday, and then sit through an afternoon lecture at Victoria's Kelburn campus. Although I had been to Wellington before, this was the first time I had had time to explore. I loved the bustling city life, the hills, the waterfront. I learnt more about the family business and got to know some of our most loyal customers.

The overseas field trip was an eye-opening experience for me, personally and professionally, witnessing first-hand the enormous opportunities and challenges in Southeast Asia. We visited universities, non-governmental organisations (NGOs), think-tanks and businesses. I discovered that a little country like New Zealand could have an outsized impact on the world. While larger countries provided hundreds of millions of dollars to build large-scale infrastructure, New Zealand played to its strengths. In Myanmar, for example, we visited a thriving cave tourism operation established with development assistance from the New Zealand government.

It was my first time in the region since we had lived briefly in Jakarta. At every juncture I found myself reflecting on how things had turned out. All those years ago I had been a child refugee living in secret in a dormitory, and now I was a New Zealand university student on a field trip.

I returned with a greater appreciation of the region, and applied for a semester abroad as I knew I wanted to go back to Asia. I listed Hong Kong, Singapore and Malaysia as my top choices. A few months later I heard that I had been accepted to the National University of Singapore.

I LANDED IN Singapore in July 2015, a couple of weeks before SG50 — the city-state's golden jubilee, celebrating 50 years of independence. It was the first time I had lived away from home and I was nervous about how I would cope, but I soon fell into a rhythm. I developed close friendships with students from around the world, all of us foreign exchange students eager to use Singapore as a base to learn about the growing importance of Asia. I joined the university rugby team but played only one game; the season was cancelled because of dangerous levels of smoke pollution from across the border. Neighbouring Indonesia was burning forests to feed the world's insatiable appetite for palm oil.

I became fascinated with Singapore's remarkable development story, from an Asian backwater to a thriving city-state of global importance. I read up on the nation-building efforts of Lee Kuan Yew and wondered if other countries and societies could emulate such a feat.

During term break I travelled around the region, including to some of the countries I had visited the previous year. I climbed Japan's Mt Fuji, explored the islands of Indonesia and Philippines, and even saw the orangutans on Borneo. I documented my journeys by writing articles for *Say Yes to Adventure*, a boutique outdoor-focused magazine based in Canterbury. My efforts even landed me a sponsorship deal with Macpac, the Christchurch-based outdoor apparel and equipment specialists.

The country that held the most fascination for me was Myanmar. They were due to hold their first democratic election in a quarter of a century and I was eager to be there to bear witness. I obtained a visa from the Myanmar embassy in Singapore, withdrew some US dollar notes, and packed my bags for Yangon. I had no real itinerary in mind, but had names of a couple of contacts from my previous visit. I arrived in Yangon in November 2015, just days before the election. I purchased a SIM card and hit the road, attending political rallies and meeting with activists working for Aung San Suu Kyi's National League for Democracy party.

I biked through the empty ten-lane highways of Nay Pyi Taw, the country's master-planned capital city. It had been built to house millions of people but only a few hundred thousand had relocated there, rendering the shining city an eerie ghost town. Many of my classmates at the Hagley Homework Club had been Burmese, from the country's ravaged Rakhine State. I was interested in the Rohingya people, but the roads into the state had been blocked to tourists. So much of what I was seeing reminded me of Afghanistan – the sectarian and ethnic tensions, the impoverishment resulting from decades of under-investment.

I still follow developments in that country closely. The recent clashes between civilians and the military and the unanswered plight of the Rohingya demonstrate that it will be a long road to peace and prosperity.

INSTEAD OF RETURNING to New Zealand at the end of the semester exchange, I travelled to the United Arab Emirates, to observe in person the tail end of the export chain from Kiwi Auto Wreckers. By sheer chance, Leni, one of my childhood friends from Riccarton Primary School, happened to be in the region at the same time, and we spent a few days with his relatives in Oman.

Mum and Dad reckoned that since I was in the vicinity, it would be rude not to pop in on relatives I had not seen since we lived in Sungjoy. They were scattered throughout Iran: an aunt in Mashhad, an uncle in Qom, and various family friends in Tehran.

I had heard and read much about Iran, and was fascinated by its history and culture. There are few countries as ancient, exotic and misunderstood. After Pakistan, Iran is home to the largest population of Afghan expatriates. More than a million Afghans are registered as living there, many without any right to work, or to receive education or government assistance. Countless more are undocumented, working in menial and seasonal cash jobs to send money home.

While in Tehran I had lunch with a cousin at one of the cafes in an upscale neighbourhood. After our waiter, a young Afghan perhaps my age, had delivered our food, I asked him to join us. His name was Mostafa and he was seventeen. He had fled to Iran nearly a year earlier, after his father and older brother (the family breadwinners) had been killed in a car bomb explosion in Kabul. With his mother and younger sister robbed of any hope of a stable income and food on the table, Mostafa had taken it upon himself to head to Europe. He scrounged together the family's life savings — mostly from his dad's taxi business and his brother's job as an English tutor — and borrowed money from neighbours for the journey. Leaving his mother and sister with his elderly uncle, he began the westward journey with a group of other breadwinners, young and old. The few friends didn't last long. One was shot by Iranian border guards, and two elderly men drowned crossing the Herat River.

With no connections in Iran, Mostafa had hoped to keep a low profile in Iran and cross into Turkey. He made it as far as Qom, the seminary that produces all of Iran's clerics. Sleeping outside a train station one night, he was beaten and robbed by a night patrol. With no money, he made his way to Tehran. Now he was saving what little money he was earning — as a waiter, a bricklayer and a cleaner — to repay what he owed his neighbours. Europe was no longer an option; even if he could get himself to Turkey, he was put off by the stories he had heard of boats sinking. His mother had seen the photo of Alan Kurdi, the Syrian toddler whose body had washed up on a Turkish beach, and urged her only son to come back home. They would make do with whatever they could. Inshallah.

Mostafa's story is of course far from unique. With

their breadwinners killed or permanently disabled in a violent attack, many families are forced to leave all they have ever known in search of an opportunity to rebuild. I was moved by his story; it reminded me of what Hussein had been through when he'd fled to Afghanistan all those years ago. As he packed down our table, I handed him a wad of cash in a handshake. His eyes lit up. I could tell he wanted to be polite and reject the offer, but we both knew the money would be life-changing for him. I held his gaze and wished him well on his journey.

I RETURNED TO New Zealand at the start of 2016 a different person. In order to help me digest everything I had learnt over my six months away, I headed into Arthur's Pass National Park with some friends. It was so refreshing to be in the Southern Alps, one of my favourite places in the world.

I had seen parts of the world I never thought I'd see. I had one more year of undergraduate studies and wondered what I would do next. Meanwhile, I was back to doing one-off jobs in the weeks before university started again. After six months of travel, my bank account was in urgent need of a boost.

It was nice to be back — I had missed my family and

friends. And we had a new addition to the Nazari clan – Sakhi was now a proud dad, and Mohanna was my first niece. Mohanna also made Mum and Dad grandparents. I had seen a photo of her when I was in Myanmar, but it was surreal to hold her in my arms. Some months later, Mohanna would be joined by another girl: Nazanin, Hussein's first-born. A year later, Shekufah would have her first child, Parisa, a cherub of a girl.

Now that they had three healthy granddaughters, I wondered if Mum and Dad ever thought about the daughter they had lost all those years ago. The birth of a baby brings renewed energy into a household, and the new grandparents were beaming with pride. Life has a way of coming full circle, and to see their children having their own families was clearly a source of great contentment.

22.
THE PROMISED LAND

THE CREW THAT watched me cross the stage at my graduation in 2016 numbered eighteen. For so many refugee parents this is what it is all about — the target they had been aiming for from the beginning. It was a glorious day and one that I will cherish for a long time.

With a degree in international relations under my belt, I was eager for some fieldwork and I knew there was no better place to start than Afghanistan. I had kept up with developments throughout my studies, and I wanted to see how things had progressed on the ground since my visit in 2012. And so in 2017 I made a return trip with both my parents.

Sungjoy looked very different. Many front gardens and

rooftops now featured solar panels, generating enough power to draw water from a newly dug well. One of my uncles had built a concrete water storage pond, which would fill up during the day and be emptied in the evening. No more midnight water runs. The communal well, on which we had been so reliant in those early years, was still a treasured resource, as many houses still lacked running water. Every morning and evening I watched families — mostly women and girls — fetching water. There are no power lines in Jaghuri, or indeed in most of Ghazni province, but those with solar panels enjoyed electricity for a few hours a night.

My uncle's place had a water-cooled air pump plugged in during these hours for a better night's sleep, but I chose to sleep on the roof, like in the old days. The blanket of stars in the highlands was just as I remembered, and truly beyond compare.

There was a patchy internet signal, and in the late afternoon, when it was early morning in Europe and Canada, I watched a few people walking around the hilltops where the signal was strongest, talking to faraway relatives. It is a weird dichotomy that in a place where crops are still harvested with a sickle, there is a 4G connection to the rest of the world.

While many families had fruit orchards and gardens,

few villagers still relied on the subsistence farming we had grown up on. Farming and agriculture were still the largest industry and employed the most people. The handful of families with a relative overseas tended to their lands with a little less worry, as remittance payments meant they did not have to cover expenses on their own.

Where people used to walk or ride a donkey to the bazaars, or to the intersections of trading routes with nomadic tribes, motorbikes now meant most things could be bought from nearby markets. Although most houses still kept animals, usually a couple of goats and cows to provide dairy products, shepherds had much smaller herds to look after.

Foreign aid, particularly from Japan and Germany, had funded the construction of a new school in Sungjoy. Boys and girls, from primary through to high-school age, travelled every day as far as 30 kilometres to learn Farsi, English and the sciences. While faith remained a central pillar of daily life, it was refreshing to see that the school curriculum had modernised significantly, and mostly done away with rote learning.

A small stretch of the provincial road had been paved, thanks to American and European development assistance, but the segments that had not yet been destroyed by explosive devices had buckled heavily, leaving deep ruts that rendered them just as impractical as before. I suspect it was a mix of overloaded trucks and poor construction, as subcontractors raced to finish a job in order to secure another generous contract. On the drive to Sungjoy we made way for two road trains, each convoy at least a hundred trailers strong, with almost every trailer ridiculously overloaded.

International development assistance still makes up the lion's share of Afghanistan's national budget. Coupled with remittances from overseas and from NGOs, foreign money had paid for the new school, an indoor sports hall, a new community hall, and the paving of the main street in the market. The initial plan had been to renovate the existing community hall, so the brand-new one was controversial. Dad and I attended a funeral there, marking the death of an elder from a nearby village. A few men I spoke to expressed their displeasure at the building of the new hall.

The main problem they saw was the declining population. Why build a magnificent hall when there is no one to fill it? Many young men had left for better opportunities in the cities. A handful had gone overseas — on academic scholarships to Turkey or India, or to work as labourers in the Persian Gulf. There was nothing to keep teenagers in the villages — no jobs, or pathways to higher education.

Although Sungjoy and surrounding villages had been spared from the heroin and methamphetamine epidemic ravaging many of the cities, I wondered how long it might be before the young men and women of villages like Sungjoy would also succumb to such desperation.

This was the second funeral in a month. A few weeks earlier there had been a large farewell procession for three soldiers who had been ambushed by the Taliban while manning a nearby watch post. In Afghanistan it seemed all the young men were either recruited, killed or pushed out – to the cities or further afield.

ANOTHER COLOSSAL ISSUE for Afghanistan is the level of corruption. Take the case of one of my uncle's business associates; let's call him Ibrahim.

Ibrahim owned a medium-sized company producing household cleaning products, most of which utilised industrial-grade alcohol. He employed about 25 staff. Because the production of alcohol is illegal in Afghanistan, Ibrahim imported alcohol from abroad, and it was trucked to Kabul from Iran or Pakistan. Once a month Ibrahim would drive to the large land port in the industrial section of Kabul to collect the order, taking a small fortune in cash to 'help lubricate the process', as he would say, paying off the port master, police and government officials along the way.

The previous year, while picking up his usual shipment, he had been detained by customs officials for 'false or forged documentation', a trumped-up charge that hung on a spelling mismatch between his government ID card and company cards. After refusing to pay the exorbitant fee demanded, Ibrahim was taken to prison.

He was released four months later after paying bribes amounting to US$300,000 – double the company's annual turnover. The money had been donated by family and community networks overseas and was paid out to officials at every level of government and across multiple provinces.

Ibrahim is the kind of citizen who could easily up and leave Afghanistan and take his wealth to India or the Gulf states, leaving dozens unemployed. Such is the choice that people have to make. It is a sad state of affairs that corruption remains one of the greatest challenges bedevilling Afghanistan. I remember one former diplomat telling us the best way would be to fire the top quarter of every government agency and replace them with trained, educated and more conscientious people. I understood the sentiment, but cutting off the head of the snake would imperil the rest of the body. Only incremental cultural change, spread across multiple generations and coupled with stronger institutions, will alleviate the problem. Corruption is an intractable problem, and no society so far has come up with a fast-track solution.

ON THE LAST day of our visit we headed to the nearest bazaar to stock up on the dried fruit and nuts I am so fond of. As Mum and Dad went from shop to shop, saying their goodbyes and picking out items requested by friends in New Zealand, I wandered down an alleyway, following the sound of stamping feet. Behind the row of shops, in a field akin to a carpark, local horse owners had gathered to sharpen their skills. Their horses danced, pranced, dashed and whinnied in a mesmerising routine. The enthusiastic crowd parted like the Red Sea as one of the riders galloped in at full pace from the far end of the field, holding aloft a short spear in one hand, reins in the other. At the last second he threw it at a clay marker, shattering it with laser precision.

It turned out a big buzkashi tournament was imminent, and these riders were practising for the skills competition. Buzkashi, Afghanistan's national sport, also known as the most dangerous sport in the world, is a chaotic and exhilarating game that involves a twelve-strong team of horse riders jostling for possession of a goat carcass. It is popular across Central Asia, tracing its roots back to the Mongol Empire — or, these locals would tell me, even further back, to the time of Alexander the Great. Western audiences were first exposed to buzkashi in the opening scenes of *Rambo III* when the title character, having never played the game before, almost beats the veteran *mujahideen* at their own game. Of course.

I noticed the riders were mostly older men and wondered if younger generations would continue the tradition. When lives are disrupted and people forced to flee, one of the first casualties is culture. Although some aspects can be picked back up or blended with other cultures, the more immaterial elements, such as poetry, craftsmanship, language and oral histories, are much harder to replace or replicate. This is profoundly more difficult when those societies are largely oral cultures. For example, Azergi, the particular dialect of Farsi spoken in villages such as Sungjoy, is a dying language.

Walking back to the market, I found Mum and Dad at a teahouse. Dad was in conversation with a skinny, bearded man a little older than me. This man, whom we will call Yosef, had grown up in a destitute family on the outskirts of Sungjoy. His parents had both died from tuberculosis, leaving Yosef and his siblings to fend for themselves at a young age.

A few years earlier, Yosef's younger brother, seeking a salary and three square meals a day, had enlisted in the Afghan National Army (ANA). Six months later he came home in a coffin. Battling mental health issues and seeking an escape from the hand he was dealt, Yosef travelled to Kabul and then on to Herat, hoping to cross the border into Iran. He made it as far as Mashhad, in eastern Iran, before he was swept up by immigration authorities. In place of detention, he was offered an attractive monthly wage if he enlisted in an Iranian-backed militia fighting the Islamic State.

Fearing the brutality of indefinite detention otherwise, Yosef enlisted and, after a short bootcamp in southern Iran, was sent to join a militia in Mosul, Iraq. Within days of his arrival, Yosef's unit was dispatched to the Iraq–Syria border — the front line. He found himself fighting alongside a bunch of other mercenaries — Russians, Chechens, Afghans, Iranians and Iraqis, all advancing into Syria.

He showed me photos and videos as he told his story. A strong-jawed Russian, machine gun at his hip, posing like Arnold Schwarzenegger in *The Terminator*. A video of himself at the helm of a heavy machine gun atop a Hilux ute, firing into the distance. Most haunting of all was a row of bodies face down in a ditch. Yosef told me they were civilians who had been executed by IS mere hours before his unit had captured the town.

After months of surviving the front line, Yosef had had enough. At the end of his rotation he collected his wages and defected, spending a significant portion of his pay on getting home. It didn't take a clinical psychologist to tell that he was suffering from the illnesses that afflict so many veterans – post-traumatic stress disorder and depression. I could see from the scars on his arms and the state of his teeth that he was probably also dabbling in heroin.

He had eventually found work as a mechanic. Although he had wanted to join the ANA, he was haunted by what happened to his brother. Yosef told me he was not optimistic about the future for Afghanistan. The Taliban, although expelled from power in 2001, were now surging back, retaking provinces that had been won back from them by the ANA and troops from the NATO-led International Security Assistance Force (ISAF).

The black flag of ISIS cast a further shadow over Afghan soil, with the establishment in 2015 of the death cult's Afghanistan chapter – the Islamic State of Khorasan (IS-K). Having experienced the brutality of IS first hand, Yosef was seriously worried about the depravity that would ensue if IS-K were allowed to thrive. He was not wrong. At the time of writing, IS-K had claimed responsibility for more than a hundred attacks across Afghanistan, killing more than 800 civilians, the overwhelming majority of them Hazara. Although smaller and more localised than the Taliban, their brand of extremism is on the rise, and poses a growing threat to peace and stability in Afghanistan.

YOSEF'S WORDS PROVED prophetic. A year after my visit, in November 2018, the Taliban launched a coordinated campaign in Jaghuri. Beyond the provincial capital of Ghazni, there is little strategic value in the region, but perhaps they wanted to send a message about their resurgence, and their ability to move in on even the safest territory. The Taliban and their sympathisers look at Jaghuri as a beacon of everything they despise: education, modernity, female empowerment and a global outlook.

Three distinct groups of Taliban-aligned militants initiated the attack by first destroying cellphone towers and ambushing watch posts manned by local militia. As word spread that they were headed to Sang Masha, the district capital, villagers from throughout the district mobilised, shouldering arms that had not seen the light of day for many years. The villagers held their ground for three days until elite ANA commandos were dispatched to the area to assist. After a week of skirmishes, the Taliban retreated.

Although the locals had won, victory had come at a heavy cost, with almost the entire unit of ANA commandos wiped out.

In 2012 the security situation in Ghazni province had been stable, but this time around it was far less so. Jaghuri was surrounded by Taliban-controlled territories. The stretch of highway connecting it to cities such as Qarabagh and Ghazni was a lawless wasteland, controlled by bandits and militants. It seemed as if the country had made no progress since we had fled in 2001. Travellers are frequently mugged. I saw many watch posts that had been abandoned, presumably after coming under a Taliban attack. As before, the wreckage of burnt cars and trucks littered the highways, only this time they were not Soviet issue.

As we left the relative safety of Jaghuri, Mum murmured a prayer under her breath. We stopped by a cemetery, the last outpost before we hit the road proper. Graves in Afghanistan are adorned with flags and ribbons that visitors kiss and touch to their forehead, uttering a prayer to the ancestors and for a safe passage. As Mum and I walked towards a flagpole we saw a group of young women around a grave. Mum greeted the women, and after only a few sentences they realised that my mum and their mum — whom they had just buried — had been childhood friends. It reminded me of the one degree of separation we are so familiar with in New Zealand. There's an old saying that goes, 'Put two Afghans in a room for ten minutes and they'll find out they know each other's grandparents.' As we left, Mum gave the young women some money and a scarf, and we were on our way.

Travelling along dirt roads, we left a trail of dust in our wake. Then, going no more than 30 kilometres an hour along ridges and through valleys, we rounded a bend at the base of a hill and came to an abrupt stop. There were about a dozen cars ahead of us, reversing away from a fuel tanker that was fully ablaze. It was the last in a convoy of supply trucks. We could see the trucking company's private security contractors atop a nearby ridge, exchanging fire with militants on the other side of the hill. We waited in our cars, with each staccato crack of automatic gunfire intensifying Mum's anxiety. Eventually ANA soldiers arrived in armoured vehicles and secured the area. After some hours the firefight was over, and the soldiers gestured that it was safe to continue. They created a detour around the burning truck and we were back on the road.

We had been lucky. Thousands of civilians in Afghanistan are killed every year — caught in crossfire, casualties of a drone strike or a military engagement, or targeted by suicide bombers. Those who survive death from flying bullets and bombs can be targeted by bandits and militants who operate kidnapping, extortion and people-trafficking rings. The UN has estimated that civilian casualties in Afghanistan in 2020 topped 10,000 killed or wounded, the sixth year in a row it had surpassed that figure. Estimates of civilian casualties are notoriously imprecise and range from 100,000 to 250,000 killed or wounded since 2001. While the majority are victims of militant forces such as the Taliban, a range of sources suggest that between a quarter to a third of civilian casualties are a result of ANA or ISAF-led operations.

On the drive back to Kabul, I thought about what Afghanistan might look like in another world, another time. In among the chaos and despair, I saw glimpses of potential. With soaring peaks and clear lakes that rival the best the South Island of New Zealand has to offer, Afghanistan is a country of spectacular and largely undiscovered natural beauty. I pictured hordes of foreign backpackers taking in the scenery of a network of world-class national parks. In winter the mountains receive a generous coating of snow, offering the prospect of superb ski fields. I imagined alpine lodges and cabins, just like in the Swiss Alps, catering to a range of holidaymakers.

Vast teams of well-trained, well-paid miners would work the numerous state-owned and privately run mining operations. In 2010 surveyors from the United States

Department of Defence estimated that a US$1 trillion motherlode of precious metals lay untouched in the Afghan hinterland — cobalt, lithium, copper and deep rich veins of iron ore and gold, resources that would be crucial in the twenty-first century. This could be the basis for a significant tax revenue for the government, highly skilled employment, and even a sovereign wealth fund.

I imagined Afghan exports catering to the global demand for premium organic foods: cherries, apricots, grapes, pomegranates, almonds, saffron and premium high-country beef and lamb. I envisaged world-class infrastructure, powered by Afghanistan's plentiful supply of renewable energy.

I imagined foreign homes adorned with high-class rugs and carpets handmade by artisans continuing centuries-old traditions of craftsmanship.

I imagined a country where everyone had a seat at the table, and women were valued for more than their domestic skills. I imagined a nation where differences in culture and language were reconciled under a common creed. A nation where the Hazara genocide was recognised.

I was still dreaming about this perfect future when we reached the main road into Kabul. A barbed-wire checkpoint was manned by ANA soldiers, with a dozen armoured vehicles parked nearby. A sudden reality check.

It will be a long time before any of my dreams are realised. But Afghanistan has made significant strides since the American invasion, and progress seemed to have accelerated since my last visit. There have been marked improvements in health, education and civic engagement, especially for women and minorities.

Primetime television when we were there featured a plethora of current affairs shows covering the day's events in multiple languages. Journalists continued to highlight social issues such as poverty, drug use, corruption and education. The two biggest stories of the day involved corruption at the Afghan Ministry of Mines, and negligence by Kabul authorities that had led to a fatal fire in a packed city market. The sports news highlighted the ongoing success of the national cricket team, and the inaugural festival of the Kabul Snowsports Club.

The most popular show was *Afghan Star*, a singing competition. Contestants performed songs in all the major languages, from classical *ghazal* to Western-style rap, often with matching outfits, ranging from colourful dresses to ripped jeans and a snapback cap. The show was incredibly popular, and viewers spent a small fortune text-voting for their chosen contestants. My cousin spent the better half of a month's wages supporting his favourite singer. (He didn't win.)

At a local gym in Kabul we ran into two of Afghanistan's brightest sports stars. One was Rohullah Nikpai, a two-time Olympic bronze medallist in taekwondo. Rohullah's story captured the world's attention when he won Afghanistan's first Olympic medal in Beijing in 2008, and repeated the feat in London in 2012. The other was Baz Mohammad 'The Afghan Eagle' Mubariz, a chiselled athlete who was a rising star in the growing mixed martial arts circuit. Thinking about these two, I wondered how many other Afghan athletes, academics and business leaders had had their dreams cut short by the war and unrest that have ravaged the country for decades.

Afghanistan is rich with talent, but poor in opportunity. While religious fundamentalism remains the raison d'être for the Taliban and similar terrorist groups, the belief system is not their only recruitment tool. Many of these fighters are not there because they are answering the call for jihad. Young men, bereft of economic opportunity and largely illiterate, are attracted by the sense of purpose and the promise of stable wages. For that, they will willingly pick up a gun, grow a beard and don a turban. This is what drove Yosef to Syria. It is why some farmers switch from growing wheat to cultivating something a lot more profitable, like opium. If these young men were educated, and offered a productive role in society, then I believe many of Afghanistan's problems would be solved. It is a simple yet proven principle that when people are able to be productive members of society, and have the means to provide for their loved ones, then that society benefits enormously. Sadly, Afghanistan is handicapped by a vicious cycle of corruption, underinvestment and instability. This is all the more frustrating given the boundless potential which remains untapped.

I left Afghanistan with few answers to my many questions. The security situation had deteriorated significantly in the five years since my first visit. An air of unease hung over the country, almost as if the nation were holding its breath. Yet I was buoyed by seeing the cadre of educated and committed activists, public servants and community leaders who were moving Afghanistan forward, determined to not repeat the mistakes of the past.

If this progress is allowed to continue, Afghanistan could finally realise its full potential.

23.

A DARK DAY IN THE GARDEN CITY

IN HIGH SCHOOL I learnt how the brain remembers minute details of traumatic experiences. The time, the place, the weather, what people were wearing, their facial expressions — all the details that generally escape us when we try to recall everyday events. Ask any Cantabrian what they were doing when the earthquakes struck, and they will recount in vivid detail the slow rumblings that jolted their lives.

And so it is with that level of detail that I recall the events of 15 March 2019 in Christchurch.

It was an overcast Friday afternoon. I had flown in from Wellington that morning to spend some time with family and catch the last of the summer sun on the

Southern Alps. Shekufah picked me up from the airport with her daughter, Parisa, in the back seat and we headed to Riccarton Mall for lunch.

I had not been home for a few months so there was a lot to catch up on. Parisa was growing up fast and Shekufah and husband Javid were settling in to married life in a new community built after the earthquakes. There is a running joke that Hazara go from driving a Toyota Hiace, the classic workhorse of every tradie, to a Toyota Hilux, a sign that business is booming. Javid had worked as a tiler with an established Christchurch company for the past three years and he had recently set up his own firm. Business was good, and I sensed that the Hilux was not far off.

We talked about Shekufah's plan to get back to work when Parisa was a little older, and the housewarming party we had been invited to that evening, when midway through lunch I received a news alert: 'BREAKING: Reports of an active shooter in Christchurch.'

My mind immediately recalled the time we were placed in lockdown at high school after reports of a man waving a gun around close to school grounds. The man had been quickly subdued, but not before the Armed Offenders Squad were called. It had all been a bit anticlimactic, so I didn't pay too much attention to this news. We went back to talking about upcoming weddings until I received another alert — the shooter had targeted a mosque in Riccarton.

I froze.

A flood of questions came to mind.

New Zealand does not have shootings — surely this can't be real?

Where are my little brothers? Friday lunchtime is a classic time to skip school, and I know Mostafa has a few friends who would be hanging around Riccarton. Dad was overseas, but I wondered if there were other family and friends at our community centre in Bishopdale.

We quickly made for the car, me frantically texting and calling my brothers. I was driving and as we got closer to Hagley Park I saw a convoy of police cars and ambulances — it took us both back to the days after the big earthquakes. The vehicles were heading in the direction of Masjid Al Noor.

I had been inside Al Noor only once. One of Dad's English tutors had invited us there for an Eid festival when we first arrived in Christchurch. I remembered the cream carpet and wood panelling, with neat arches on one wall. Our primary school inter-school sports league had been held across the road at Hagley Park, and often we had got off the bus in front of Al Noor. The golden dome of the mosque gleamed in the crisp winter afternoon as schoolchildren from across Canterbury gathered for afternoon sports.

A row of police cars blocked Deans Avenue and an officer was rolling out caution tape. I got out of the car and told Shekufah to drive straight home. I snuck under the tape and headed for a small crowd of bystanders, many of whom had emerged from a nearby office building. I spoke with a couple of Somali friends I'd met plenty of times on the football field. An Egyptian girl I recognised from high school stood nearby.

We talked about what we knew, but it wasn't much. At this point there were no confirmed deaths or injuries, and we had no idea of the carnage that was unfolding. Everyone was glued to their phones. Soon, speculation and rumour were spreading like wildfire.

'There are multiple shooters.'

'It's a coordinated attack; they're going for the hospital and local schools next.'

'My friend at the university just heard a large explosion.'

'My brother's high school is in lockdown and apparently there was a shooter at the gate.'

By now, media crews had arrived. A worker from the office block brought out bottles of water and packets of biscuits. My mind shot back to the biscuits and water we were given when we boarded the *Tampa*.

After some tense minutes, groups of people began to emerge from the direction of Al Noor, about a hundred metres away. I will never forget how they looked: pale-faced projections of utter horror. As if the images of what they had seen had been imprinted on their eyeballs and they were watching a never-ending horror film.

A few of the Somali boys joined me in handing out water to the people coming towards us – from between cars and behind hedges, over fences. When the shooting had started, people had apparently run out of the *masjid* and hid wherever they found safety.

But they didn't want our water; they wanted to use our phones. We handed them over and they began to call loved ones.

Men and women were now running towards the police as fast as their shocked bodies could carry them. It is customary to take off your shoes when entering a *masjid*, so many were barefoot.

One man in particular stood out. He was older, and dressed in a white shirt that matched his silver beard. I looked down and thought I saw henna on his feet – some South Asians are fond of this practice. Then I looked more closely and saw that it was not henna – it was blood. His feet, right up to the hem of his pants, were soaked in crimson. When he turned around to talk to a journalist, I saw splashes of blood right up his trouser legs.

We were convinced there must have been fatalities.

The last time I had seen such fear on a man's face was on board the *Palapa* during the storm.

We continued to try to help the people running to us from the *masjid*. One man was pushing himself in a wheelchair. I lifted the cordon tape as he rolled past me, head down. I offered him some water and my phone. He said a polite thank you and was on the phone immediately. A few moments later a young woman came running from behind me and fell at his feet. He held her with one arm as the other clutched the phone to his ear.

I couldn't make out the conversation, and was distracted anyway by the cheers and tearful relief all around me.

A man was on the phone to his mum, who was safe at the other end of Deans Ave.

A boy was on the phone to his sister, who was at the hospital with only minor injuries.

I looked back at the man in the wheelchair to see if he had heard similarly good news.

He was silent, listening intently. Suddenly the woman who had been leaning on the man's shoulder dropped to the ground in a heap. Her deep, piercing screams drew everyone's attention.

Now we knew for sure.

I allowed them a moment and then went over to them.

'I'm sorry for your loss. Is there anything I can do, Uncle?' I asked, not knowing who had been taken from him.

He didn't reply. He looked at his hands and back at me. Calm. Still as a statue. The young woman's distressed wails had wound down to heavy sobs.

'Would you like to leave this place? I could take you home, or to the hospital?' I had completely forgotten Shekufah had taken the car.

'Yes, that would be great, thank you,' he said. 'Here, take her car keys. Darling, tell me where you parked so this man can get the car and take us home,' he whispered to the woman, who was still on the ground. I later discovered she was his niece.

She hesitated, taking stock. Then she fossicked in her purse, pulled out a bunch of keys and pointed behind me, describing her car. I hurried away and found it parked on the footpath.

A police officer at the checkpoint allowed me through. I helped the man out of his wheelchair and folded it into the boot. The niece climbed in the back seat, covering her puffy eyes with her headscarf.

'To Hoon Hay, please,' said the man.

His house had a sign on the door: Hoon Hay Homeopathy. I jumped over the fence and went to the shed to fetch the spare keys. I opened the door and helped the man inside while his niece disappeared to her room. Not knowing what to do, yet not wanting to leave them alone, I hovered in the doorway. He invited me into the lounge, asking if I wanted tea. I declined and sat down on the couch, gazing at the enormous bookshelf filled with leather-bound textbooks that were bulkier than my spelling bee dictionary.

The man sat motionless in his wheelchair. Loud wailing came from the bedroom.

I introduced myself as Abbas, originally from Afghanistan.

'I thought so — you have the features of many of my Hazara friends. My name is Farid Ahmed. Today I lost my wife, Husna.'

I didn't know what to say.

'Many years ago,' he continued, 'my family and I were driving through beautiful Nelson when I was struck by a car. The driver had not been paying attention and I was dragged underneath the car and along the road. I was in hospital for some weeks, and although the doctors did their best, I lost the use of my legs. I was angry. I felt a deep, vengeful anger like hot coals. It weighed on me for many years. Why me? Why such punishment? I asked of God.'

He gazed at one spot on the carpet, eyes glassy.

'I found no answers, and it is no wonder, for I was

blind with rage. But over time, I realised that this was a test from God. I needed to let go and forgive the man who did this to me. It wasn't a punishment. When I learnt this, and forgave the man, it was as if a weight had lifted off my chest. Now God is testing me — testing us all — again today. I cannot carry the burden of anger and rage again. I forgive this man for what he has done today. I forgive his actions, even if he took away my beautiful wife.'

I was stunned. This was mere hours after the killer had stormed the *masjid*. I understood being virtuous and turning the other cheek, but I couldn't fathom how he could say he forgave the man who had brutally slain his wife, as well as countless other members of his community.

Then Farid Ahmed's fortitude quietly crumbled, and tears flowed down his face. He wiped his face with his scarf and picked up a ringing phone.

Family members began arriving by the carload, and concerned neighbours checked in as the news spread. He spoke to each of them with stoicism and grace, comforting them as if they had lost their life partner.

Eventually I called Mojtaba to pick me up. I hugged Farid goodbye, not knowing if I would see him again. He said a quiet thank you.

By now we knew that multiple people had been slaughtered by a lone gunman. I broke down in the car as

Mojtaba drove home, crying like I had never cried before. I kept imagining the terror those people must have felt in their last moments. It reminded me of that night on the *Palapa*, when everyone thought they were facing imminent death.

Had it been slow and painful for the worshippers, or was it a quick execution? How many had witnessed friends and loved ones dying? It was so close to home. What if the killer knew of the Afghan community hall and chose to unleash further terror there? Everyone I had grown up with and relied upon my whole life could have been taken out in one fell swoop.

I COLLECTED MYSELF and headed to the housewarming dinner I'd been invited to that night, arriving late. There was only one topic of conversation. Many people were scared and vowed not to return to our community hall unless armed guards were stationed outside. Some proposed safety measures such as an extra exit and wider corridors. Someone pointed out that an extra door would be no use if a killer came in with a bomb. It was a horrific conversation to be having.

We were all shocked at the brazenness of it all. The terrorist had mounted the deadliest shooting in modern

New Zealand history in broad daylight. How had the gunman got his hands on automatic weapons in New Zealand? Why were the intelligence services unaware?

This was the sort of thing we had travelled half the world to get away from. In recent years, Taliban and IS-K militants in Afghanistan had progressed from random attacks to targeting mosques, ordinary people's ultimate sanctuary. This gunman had clearly adopted this tactic in order to deliver the cruellest blow.

Some took comfort in the fact that the killer was Australian and not a New Zealander.

We were in awe that Prime Minister Jacinda Ardern, in her address to the nation that afternoon, had specifically labelled it a terrorist attack, using a term that had previously been exclusively applied to brown Middle Easterners. Many applauded the speedy police response — they had apprehended the gunman within nineteen minutes of being alerted. It could have been so much worse.

As the night wore on, the conversation focused on why the gunman had targeted the Muslim community. Everyone was acutely aware of how the events of 9/11 and the resulting War on Terror had created hostility and open resentment towards people from the Middle East. Islamophobia was a daily struggle for bearded brown males and hijab-wearing females throughout the West.

Although New Zealand had been spared the brutal excesses that became common in Europe and North America, everyone present that night could recall at some stage being called upon to answer for every Middle Easterner following a terrorist attack, having to persuade their fearful colleagues that they were different. Curious workmates and customers at shops would ask what they thought of the attack, gauging their support or otherwise. We would denounce the attackers and, if it wasn't obvious already, explain that the extremists did not represent us. That in fact these were the very people from whom we had fled.

Now perhaps every Australian — or every white person — could denounce this killer and tell us all how ashamed they were to be linked to him in any way.

An older man, a fellow *Tampa* refugee, reminded us all that when we arrived at Auckland Airport from Nauru, immigration officials had bundled us all onto buses and closed the curtains, for fear that there would be protests against our arrival. In fact only one protester had turned up with his miserable sign. We have a choice, the *Tampa* man said now. Do we choose to remember the one person who went out of his way to spoil the party, or the countless people who have helped and welcomed and supported our community since?

As shocking as the attack had been, it did not represent the New Zealand we had made home. Rebutting the divisive hatred of the gunman in the days that followed were countless neighbours, colleagues and classmates who shared the burden of our grief. They were the real New Zealand. A community that had just lost its innocence, in a shocking manner, would pick itself up and carry on. This was proven over the coming days, weeks and months.

The following day, distant neighbours came over with cards, flowers, chocolates and baking. They just knew us as the family down the road but knew we would be affected somehow. Mum, who didn't want to go outside in the days immediately following the attack, was grateful for the support. She found strength in these random acts of kindness.

Memorial services happened spontaneously around Christchurch and throughout the country. I watched on television as hundreds and thousands of people, from schoolkids to grandparents, from all ethnicities and backgrounds, paid their respects. There were powerful haka from different school groups to mourn classmates who had been slain. Even the Mongrel Mob and Black Power gangs came out to show solidarity, performing a spine-tingling haka. I remember one foreign journalist asked me which rugby team they represented. It was the first time I had laughed all week.

WITHIN HOURS OF the attack a contact centre was set up at nearby Hagley College — the classrooms we had used for the Homework Club were now filled with local and central government officials. The death toll climbed with every passing hour. Twenty, 30, 40. By week's end, we knew there were 51 dead and 40 others injured. Every affected family was given a liaison officer who would pass on official updates from the crime scene, including, crucially, in relation to body recovery.

Chefs dished out hundreds of meals twice a day. The school cafeteria was converted to a meeting hall just in time for a phalanx of MPs to arrive. I watched as the headscarf-wearing Prime Minister and representatives of all the major political parties paid their respects and promised to move swiftly to ensure the road to recovery was as smooth as possible. To this day, I am amazed at how quickly the wheels of government can turn when they have to. Countless dedicated government employees in all departments worked overtime to help ease the community's pain. I am sure that in time, New Zealand's response to this tragedy will become a textbook example of how to respond to a crisis.

The next day I visited the Memorial Park Cemetery in Linwood where the first of many funerals would take place. One of the victims had been Hajji Daoud, who arrived in New Zealand in the late 1980s. He had fled Afghanistan in his twenties, after the Soviet invasion, and made his way to Europe where he became a deckhand on merchant ships. He sailed the seas for many years before disembarking in Auckland. Hajji Daoud was one of the first Afghan residents in New Zealand, and over the years he became a conduit for many other Afghan arrivals.

When we first arrived in Christchurch there were only a handful of other families, and Hajji Daoud became a close friend to Dad. Hajji Daoud had experienced the highs and lows of the immigrant experience, and he had faced it all alone. When we arrived in Christchurch, he was eager to offer his guidance, taking the men of our community under his wing. Standing at his prayer service, I recalled sitting next to Dad at an Eid celebration in the early years as Hajji Daoud spoke of the need to preserve some parts of our Afghan heritage and drop others. He was the first person killed at the Linwood Islamic Centre. His last words had been the customary 'Hello, brother' as he welcomed the gunman, thinking he was a fellow worshipper.

I thought about my friend Naz and his family. His father, Amman, was the man who had given me the sweet onboard the *Palapa*. He had been a teacher in his village, but as a solo asylum seeker, he was sent to Nauru. After three years in the island prison, he was finally accepted to

New Zealand. He attended English classes at PEETO and drove a taxi on the weekends. Amman was a man of many talents and we used to go over to his house to get haircuts.

After receiving his citizenship, he applied to bring his wife and children to New Zealand. I first met Naz, his eldest son, when he joined our Sunday school classes; I remember being annoyed that he was better at reading than I was.

Then on 5 December 2008, while driving two teenage boys into town in his taxi, Amman was robbed at knifepoint and stabbed to death.

Perhaps the killers, drunk from a heavy night, looked at Amman's slim build and decided he would be an easy target. Or perhaps they didn't like this foreign-sounding driver looking at their drunk faces in the rear-view mirror. I vividly remember Ali waking me up the next morning to tell me the news. I assumed he had come over to kick a ball around, but when he told me what had happened, a dark cloud instantly came over me.

There is a beautiful photo taken at Amman's funeral, with his gilded casket in front of a line of community members. Everyone stood together, heads bowed as many of them had done on those days aboard the *Tampa*.

The name Amman translates to 'trust and protection' and he was now joined by dozens of other community members taken too soon.

THE NEXT DAY I received a text from Mike McRoberts, a Christchurch local and longtime anchor on *Newshub*. He wanted me to co-host a nationally televised broadcast of the *azaan*, the call to prayer, to mark one week after the attack. I borrowed a suit from a friend, and we went live. Standing on the media stage, I could see the worshippers assembling in neat rows as the call to prayer rang out from the loudspeaker. The last time I had heard the words echo beyond a *masjid* was in Sungjoy, and now it was being broadcast around an entire Western nation as supporters came together in their tens of thousands to show solidarity with the community that had been hit by this appalling tragedy. Mum, who was in the crowd with her friends, was stunned to see so many Kiwi women wearing headscarves just like her. If she had had any reluctance to go outside, she needn't worry any more.

THE ATTACK NATURALLY brought questions about racism to the fore. Suddenly, Kiwis were confronted with the uncomfortable thought that perhaps this little Antipodean paradise was not as egalitarian as it thought it was, that perhaps there was an underbelly of bigotry and violence. Talkback radio and media featured wall-to-wall discussion of what it meant to be Kiwi now that we had 'lost our innocence'.

I thought about my own experiences with racism. I had worked in many service jobs, from checkout operator to selling menswear at a mall to working in real estate, and I had never had any prejudice directed at me. My older siblings had also worked as checkout operators, interacting with hundreds of different people a week. None of us had ever been harassed or racially abused in any way.

Then it dawned on me that perhaps we benefited from a privilege that other minorities don't have. With our fluent Kiwi accents, strong tan in summer and paler skin in winter, we easily pass as locals. It could be a whole different story for people who don't blend in as easily.

Rather than point fingers at our fellow citizens, I think the real problem sits with how politicians manipulate race and racial issues for their own means, especially during an election campaign.

To my mind, it is undeniable that the Christchurch massacre had its roots in the race-baiting and demonisation of foreigners, particularly those from the Middle East, by political elites. Many politicians have built their careers on the backs of 'othering', dehumanising people who are not like them. The overt and sustained denigration of people who look, talk and worship differently certainly fuelled the Christchurch gunman's hatred towards those worshippers.

As countless politicians to the far right of politics

in Australia, the UK, Europe and the US condemned the Christchurch attack, I wondered if any of them felt complicit. While it is true that the Christchurch gunman was a 'lone wolf', his actions represented the extreme end of an ethno-nationalism that is sweeping across liberal democracies, largely on the back of economic anxiety and migration.

I was struck by the national conversation around racism. Many were quick to point to a host of things that needed changing, or the issues they said were hidden in plain sight. Although I found some of the issues worth unpacking, I was also taken by the level of hysteria attached. Some commentators called for Canterbury's Crusaders rugby team to change their name, as it was a direct reference to the medieval Christian Crusades against Islam. I felt this argument completely missed the mark, and unnecessarily denigrated an icon of the city from which many Cantabrians, myself included, drew strength and identity.

Others were even more sweeping, arguing that the entire country had a dark and ugly underbelly of racism and persecution. But this ignores the decades of solid progress in race relations that put New Zealand way ahead of any other country in this area. In the heat of such debate, the discourse becomes inflamatory, and at a moment where unity should be the prevailing theme, communities stand divided. The issue of race is a complex web of competing elements — cultural, economic and geographic to name a few — intersecting at an individual, local and systemic level. As such, discussion and policy around racial issues require tremendous patience and the courage to see the world through multiple lenses. Sadly, such nuances are often lost or blatantly ignored in order to fit a certain narrative. This is done by actors on all sides of the political spectrum, be it inadvertent, ill-informed, or with ill-intent. On the quest to realise this land of milk and honey for all, we mustn't lose sight of the journey so far. It is certainly not mission accomplished, but society has come a very long way.

24.
SABBA —
TOMORROW

WHEN I LANDED in Washington DC on 15 August 2019, the *Washington Post* had a feature marking 400 years since the arrival of the *White Lion*. This was an English pirate ship that docked at Point Comfort, Virginia in August 1619, loaded with captured Africans. The trade in human lives that developed thereafter would alter the course of world history. I thought about how it must have been for those people to be forced out of their homes and crammed into the bowels of a vessel that journeyed far across the open seas to a strange land.

As I walked around the National Mall, taking in my new surroundings, I tried to process how I had come to this point.

In my final year at the University of Canterbury I met Genevieve. We were doing the same courses and we hit it off instantly. After a summer road-tripping through the South Island, I knew we had something special. We both moved to Wellington, having accepted jobs in the public service. I began as a policy analyst at the Treasury, while she joined the Ministry of Defence.

We quickly settled into a new rhythm, exploring the North Island while developing a new circle of friends. After my last trip to Afghanistan in 2017, I returned to Wellington with renewed certainty that New Zealand would be my home for the foreseeable future. I bought an apartment in the central city, scraping the deposit together with the help of moonlighting shifts as an Uber driver. I would work a full week at the Treasury, then drive on Friday and Saturday nights. On Saturdays I would go to Kiwi Auto Wreckers and get stuck in packaging orders, stacking tyres and dealing to the mountain of paperwork that had piled up over the week. The family business was booming, and on more than one occasion I considered trading my view of the Beehive for a role at the yard. I could be a trucker just like Dad, I reckoned.

But Mum and Dad were adamant that the family business would manage just fine, and that they hadn't crossed the oceans to see me drive trucks for a living. They urged me to think bigger. As one of the crop of recent graduates, they hoped I could open doors for Mojtaba and Mostafa's generation.

On those lonely nights driving drunk partygoers home to the Hutt Valley and beyond, I couldn't help wonder what else was out there. My semester in Singapore had been a period of immense growth, and I always imagined doing something else similar if the opportunity presented itself.

I also thought about the letter I had received on my last day of high school from the Harvard student who rated my prospects there. I began talking to a few mentors, and gradually I was persuaded to apply for a Fulbright scholarship for postgraduate study at an American university. It was a golden ticket! I knew I wanted to throw my hat in the ring.

In my application letter I wrote the following:

> My philosophy in life is simple. That things aren't as bad as one imagines them to be, and that a little perspective goes a long way. I think going through any formative experience imbues the adventurer with a broader perspective on life. They say that you are the sum of all your experiences. I believe this is true for me. I am always grateful to wake up in a country where we are given the opportunity

to pursue our full potential. I remember my primary school principal saying 'most people avoid opportunity because it is dressed in overalls and looks like work'. I think this saying accurately captures my perspective on life.

After a strenuous interview process I made it to the final round. A couple of weeks later I received a call telling me I was one of the dozen successful applicants. I was as chuffed as I had been during the standing ovation after my TEDx talk.

Things started moving at pace. With the help of Fulbright New Zealand, I applied to a number of colleges in the US with international relations programmes. One by one, the offers came in. Congratulations from the University of California at Berkeley. We are delighted to welcome you to Columbia University. George Washington University welcomes you to the nation's capital. The University of Texas looks forward to welcoming you to campus in the fall. My head couldn't fit through the door any more.

I flew to Auckland to sit the academic admissions test. Unhappy with my first effort, I had another go and got a more respectable score.

The biggest challenge was getting a US student visa.

My New Zealand passport should have made it a breeze, but as is often the case with a name and travel history like mine, it was not so straightforward. I found myself trapped in a legal and bureaucratic web.

My visa application was submitted in the time after the Supreme Court upheld the Trump administration's Muslim ban in July 2018, and before the federal government shut down in December 2018. When I heard nothing back for months I assumed it got lost in the paper maze. Meanwhile, all of my fellow Fulbrighters received their visas.

While I was waiting for my visa, March 15 happened. It seemed to have come out of nowhere, but with the global increase in white supremacist terrorism I knew it would not be the last such attack. I wanted to learn more about this movement, and being on the ground in the US would provide the ideal learning environment.

The Security Studies Program at Georgetown University's School of Foreign Service in Washington DC offered exactly what I was looking for. As if to reinforce this fact, two weeks before I arrived, a white supremacist had opened fire in a busy mall in Texas in a targeted attack on the Hispanic community.

MY TIME IN Washington has been marked by extraordinary ironies and juxtapositions. Although it is an openly liberal city, at odds with the policies of the recently departed president, the growing number of asylum seekers at the southern US border dominated news coverage and there was constant rivalry in the media over whose headline could scream the loudest:

> *Kids in Cages*
> *Crisis at the Border*
> *Caravans of Asylum Seekers with Potential ISIS Militants*

It was eerily reminiscent of the *Tampa* saga, only this time I was on the outside looking in. I could understand the need for an orderly immigration system, but in such a supercharged political atmosphere there was no room for nuance. The voters who shouted 'Build the Wall' were the same farmers and fishermen who could not fill vacancies on their farms and trawlers.

To my mind, at the crux of the hysteria surrounding immigration is a deep-rooted fear of the powerful forces of globalisation which have upended the America that many grew up in. With jobs being shipped offshore, and once industrious towns being hollowed out, there is little room for empathy. The majority of Americans are too busy trying to put food on the table and pay health insurance to have a moment's care for the downtrodden, the tired, the sick. This is not their fault. They are not heartless, or racist, or fascist, as some liberal commentators and critical race theorists attest.

Washington is a bubble. The Washington metro area and its surrounding counties have the highest average household income in the country. I lived in Arlington, a 15-minute walk across the river from Georgetown's main campus and rated as the most liveable city in the entire United States. One only needs to travel a couple hours into rural America to witness the vast patchwork quilt of people and politics of American society. With Genevieve, who joined me in Washington, I have visited more than twenty states, and I can now appreciate why a poor, uneducated, single mother living in a trailer home in rural America might have a *Make America Great Again* bumper sticker. The triple forces of the Covid-19 pandemic, social unrest and an economic meltdown within the space of a few months in 2020 revealed the extent of this country's challenges. Americans, already crushed under the weight of numerous insecurities, felt the rug pulled from under them, revealing the rot that has set into the foundations of their country. American exceptionalism laid bare. I remain optimistic that the American experiment will continue, as it has for centuries. But for now, it is abundantly clear that for a majority of Americans, the American Dream remains just that — a dream.

ON MORE THAN one occasion I would have to pinch myself as I walked across Georgetown's leafy campus. Here was the son of a truck driver and homemaker from the mountains of Afghanistan, walking to attend class at one of the most prestigious universities in the world. I felt an indescribable and potent mix of emotions. Dad's gamble had paid off, and I was enjoying the rewards. It was now on me to honour the hard work of my parents, and to build on the foundations they had set.

As I got stuck in to my classwork, I developed a strong interest in events back in Afghanistan. After two decades of conflict, US policy had come full circle. In late 2001, when they ousted the Taliban, Washington made the mistake of consigning these militants to the dustbin of history. This was compounded when the White House turned its attention to Iraq. Slowly, the Taliban rebuilt in the shadows of democratic Afghanistan, and were now stronger than ever.

Twenty years later, Washington wished to bring the Taliban to the negotiating table, a move it could well have made back in 2001. In a plush hotel in Qatar in February 2020 representatives of the American government and the Taliban signed a peace deal, paving the way for an American withdrawal and the possibility of the Taliban directly negotiating with the government in Kabul. Sitting in Washington, I was captivated by these events.

Following the signing of the peace deal, the Taliban began a campaign of targeted killings of the country's best and brightest. Journalists, lawyers, government employees, students, anyone who could help raise the country's fortunes. It was a surgically precise campaign calculated to bring the government in Kabul to its knees.

At the same time, IS-K continued its bloody sectarian war against Afghanistan's minorities. Every life taken reminded me of how different mine could have been. While I wrote this book, IS-K conducted more than two dozen attacks, claiming the lives of hundreds of innocent Afghans and injuring thousands more, the vast majority of them Hazara. In August 2019 a suicide bombing at a Hazara wedding killed at least 63 and injured over 200, wiping out entire families. In March 2020 an attack on a Hazara procession commemorating a Shi'a nationalist killed 32. Two weeks later, IS-K militants attacked a Sikh temple, killing at least 25.

Perhaps the most sickening attack occurred in May

2020 in the maternity ward of a Kabul hospital. The attack on the Doctors Without Borders facility, located in the Hazara-majority neighbourhood of Dasht-e-Barchi, Kabul, an area that is unfortunately very used to violence, claimed the lives of 24 mothers and newborns. IS-K militants stormed the corridors of the hospital, heading straight to the distinctive pink and purple walls of the maternity ward. Exactly a year later, in May 2021, the same militants set off a series of car bombs outside a girls' primary school in the same neighbourhood, claiming the lives of more than 100 schoolgirls, and injuring 150 others. In Afghanistan, the smallest coffins are the heaviest.

Although every killing was brutal, the November 2020 attack at Kabul University felt too close to home. IS-K militants had stormed the campus, setting off suicide bombs and shooting indiscriminately into a lecture hall, killing 32 students and injuring 50. Students were gunned down as they hid under desks. As Georgetown's enchanting campus took on the vibrant colours of autumn, blood was being spilled in Kabul. *That could have been me*, I thought. By targeting schools, hospitals and places of worship, the militants seek to destroy the hard-won achievements of the past two decades. For the militants, a girl attending school or a young man with a book is a greater threat to their ideology than any bullet or missile. Afghanistan, and more precisely the Hazara community, experiences a terrorist attack equivalent to the March 15 massacre almost on a weekly basis. The ferocity and frequency of the bloodshed is a sledgehammer to the chest of so many innocent families, and a key driver of the continued displacement of the Afghan people. When I see the faces of grieving mothers and fathers, I feel a burning rage searching for an outlet. Who is to blame? The elected government in Kabul for its inability to protect its citizens, especially the Hazara? The Americans for the ill-fated War on Terror? The mullahs and madrassas that peddle in militant sectarianism? Or maybe, it is the fault of the Afghan people, for simply being cursed with misfortune? Amidst the fog of war, and buried in the rubble, a million questions remain unanswered. Sadly, one thing is certain. By the time this book reaches your hands, there will have been countless more attacks, claiming the lives of even more innocent Afghans.

AS THE PROTESTS and riots sparked by the police slaying of George Floyd raged across cities in America and beyond, Floyd's last words, 'I can't breathe', became a battle cry for the movement against police brutality and racial injustice. Lost in the cacophony was a similar cry from Afghans. On the opposite side of the world, a different plea for help sparked a similar movement against injustice — *Sokhtam!* 'I'm burning!'

The plea came from a young Afghan boy as he crawled from a burning car in Yazd province, central Iran. A harrowing minute-long video shows the badly burnt boy pleading for help — *Sokhtam!* The car he was in had exploded in flames after allegedly being shot at by Iranian police. Three people were killed in the inferno, with five more hospitalised. A second video shows the survivors, with at least one victim handcuffed to a hospital bed.

Within hours these videos spread across social media platforms, sparking outrage in Afghanistan and in diaspora communities around the world. It was only weeks after another deadly encounter on Iranian soil in May 2020, when up to 45 Afghan migrants were allegedly drowned by Iranian border guards.

In Washington DC one Sunday afternoon in June 2020, some 200 protesters, the majority of whom were part of the vast Afghan diaspora, gathered outside the Afghan embassy (Iran has no diplomatic presence in the US) to voice their outrage. Speeches decried the numerous human rights violations Afghan refugees continue to suffer at home and abroad.

IT IS EASY to be consumed by all the terrible atrocities being committed in Afghanistan, and against Afghans around the world. I think about 'what if' scenarios for Afghanistan. What if US special forces had captured Osama bin Laden in the mountains of Tora Bora just months after 9/11? What if the US$2 trillion spent on the longest war in American history had been put to better use? What if the Afghan people put all their differences aside in the face of a common enemy? These questions offer little insight to the future, and I find myself weighed down with hopelessness, seeing only a dark future for that country. But this is tempered by glimmers of hope, sparked by Afghans who have battled against all odds and won. Hope is what drives the human spirit, and there are countless examples of Afghans charging ahead in spite of their circumstances. This indefatigable drive is truly inspiring.

Take, for example, the Afghan girls' robotic team, comprising a bunch of scrappy village girls who were denied visas to a robotics competition in the US, only to sweep the competition in Europe. They would later use their skills to build low-cost ventilators during the Covid-19 pandemic.

Or Fatima Sultani, who, at the age of eighteen, became the youngest Afghan woman to climb Mt Noshaq, which at a mighty 7492 metres is Afghanistan's highest peak. Her mother endured years of wearing an all-body burqa and never leaving the home without a male chaperone, yet her daughter has her sights set on Mt Everest.

Or Zarifa Ghafari, a fearless public official who, at 26, became one of Afghanistan's first female mayors. There have been numerous assassination attempts against her, the latest claiming her father, but she continues to stand as a proud flagbearer for the next generation of Afghan leaders.

Or Saad Mohseni, an Afghan refugee who left the comforts of an investment banking career in Australia to establish Afghanistan's most popular news and entertainment channel, Tolo.

But perhaps the story that best captures the essence of Afghanistan over the last twenty years is that of Shamsia Alizada, who was born a year after the Taliban were toppled. Her family had moved from their mountain village to Kabul because her parents believed education for their children would enable them to take part in the promise of a new Afghanistan. Midway through high school, Shamsia was almost killed in an attack on her school that claimed the lives of dozens of her classmates.

In 2020 this coalminer's daughter topped the national university entrance exams, ahead of nearly 200,000 other students.

Shamsia's story is the unfulfilled promise of Afghanistan. I wonder how many similar stories are cut short by shrapnel or buried under a mountain of misery. Such is daily life in Afghanistan.

I don't want to downplay the challenges ahead: reality for many Afghans is dire and I do not know what the future holds. But I refuse to believe there is no hope. Progress — however slow, however fragile — is progress. Afghanistan has long been a tortured country, but I find solace and hope in the potential that will be unleashed when peace is finally achieved.

MY FATHER HAS many sayings that he employs to good effect. One of his favourites is a parable involving water. When he was a young man walking along a riverbank, he came to a spot where the land dropped a few metres, with the water descending as a small waterfall. He examined the rocks beneath and noted how, over time, the flow of water had smoothed and shaped the rocks like clay on a potter's wheel. Beside the main curtain of the waterfall, a small rivulet of water no thicker than a pencil had carved out the rock beneath it into a perfect bowl. Had it not been so heavy, I suspect Dad might have taken it home as a water bowl for his cows. He never stopped marvelling at how a mere trickle of water, slight yet persistent, had beaten a rock into submission.

When I went back to Afghanistan for the first time, I retold this story to a class at Loman High School. In my stilted Farsi, I said the rock represents all of the challenges that stand in the way of this generation of Afghans. The rock may seem solid and immovable at first, but gradually, with dogged determination, the water will find a way.

I told them about the impossible odds we had faced in leaving our home in search of a better tomorrow. I spoke of boarding up our house and leaving with no idea where we would end up, of risking life and limb on a perilous journey, of travelling halfway across the planet in search of a foreign land that did not want us, of starting from scratch with nothing but the clothes on our backs, and of navigating the space between two worlds. The rock we faced had seemed as insurmountable as a mountain. And yet here I stood.

Just as the creek, the life source of the village, had carved the valley on its journey from the mountains, we were also on a journey. This was our story — an endless search for a better tomorrow.

EPILOGUE

WE LIVE AND die by the stories we share. The story of those rescued by the *Tampa* is still being written but for my family, so far, it has had a happy ending.

In writing this book I have tried to provide some insight into what happened to one family whose lives were uprooted, who undertook a perilous journey to safety and survival, and who thrived given the opportunity.

Countless refugees around the world are not nearly so lucky. I personally know of a dozen families whose lives are on hold in Indonesia, Iran, Turkey and Pakistan. There are many more stories like mine, each as challenging and engaging as the last. You could replace the Hazara with Rohingya, Yazidis or Uyghur. The struggles and oppression they face are depressingly similar.

I know the issue of boat people is divisive. Nobody, myself included, wants to see boat after boat full of refugees fleeing their homelands and seeking safe harbour somewhere — anywhere. I have been through the experience and would not wish it on anybody — it is a desperate and terrifying ordeal.

Nobody wants to see bodies washed ashore in a repeat of the tragedy of SIEV X, the Indonesian fishing boat en route to Australia that capsized in international waters on 19 October 2001, killing 353 people.

Nobody wants to see the heart-breaking images of the body of three-year-old Syrian Alan Kurdi cast up on a beach.

And neither am I advocating for countries to take in the millions of refugees around the world. Even if every signatory to the Refugee Convention were to increase its refugee intake tenfold, it would hardly make a dent in the more than 70 million displaced peoples around the world.

Europe is already creaking under the weight of asylum seekers, and recent election results in many countries show dangerous splits emerging over the refugee issue and support for granting asylum.

The focus must be remedying the root cause of the refugees' displacement, be it civil conflict or climate change. This is a lofty demand, as these challenges look set to worsen in the short to medium term.

Ethiopia may be the next tinder box. Home to more than 100 million people, the country has seen growing civil unrest and open conflict between various ethnic and political factions. If it continues to be left unaddressed, it is possible that millions of Ethiopians will be displaced, and hundreds of thousands may attempt to cross the Mediterranean Sea.

It is incumbent on the international community, through such organisations as the African Union, the European Union, the United Nations, individual nation states and various NGOs, to step up and show leadership in addressing the open wounds of social upheaval and tribal politics around the world. There is a strong temptation to conclude that these ancient feuds are not the problem of the 'civilised' West, as the flames of ethnic tension can never fully be put out. It is even easier to look away from the problems afflicting foreign faces and places, as if the residents of distant lands are too far from the reach of help. I can understand these sentiments better than most as I have lived in both worlds. Climate change will be the biggest driver of human displacement worldwide and the duty of responsibility is on much of the developed world, given the disproportionate impact of climate change. We are seeing this already, as low-lying Pacific Islands such as Kiribati consider permanent emigration as a means of future-proofing their civilisation. As this challenge draws near, it will be increasingly harder to turn a blind eye to the suffering.

If it is not clear already, I consider myself incredibly fortunate to have been resettled in New Zealand. Had Prime Minister Helen Clark not made the offer to take in the families from the *Tampa*, my life would have been very different. The offshore detention camps are inhumane and belittle Australia in the eyes of the world, just as the situation at Guantanamo Bay has injured America's global reputation. It is comforting to see that the number of detainees has dropped significantly over the years but, sadly, Australia's hardline message to asylum seekers remains unchanged. In recent years, attention has turned to forcibly deporting Asian families who have breached their visa conditions, at the cost of tens of millions of dollars to taxpayers. This is an extension of the same politics that inspired offshore detention. This is a cynical approach, given that there are more than 70,000 visa overstayers in Australia at any time.

In 2018 I was asked to front the 'Kids off Nauru' campaign by World Vision New Zealand. It was a social media campaign aimed at getting children out of the detention centre in Nauru; some of them had been born there and spent their entire lives behind razor wire. I am proud to say that there are no children currently in detention in Nauru.

It is a small victory, but an important one. I am confident that with sustained pressure, Australia's offshore detention camps will eventually be closed for good. Whether Australia's political reputation will ever recover is another issue.

The refugee crisis is a global challenge. I hope this book has shed some light on the issue and dispelled the misconceptions regarding refugees.

ACKNOWLEDGEMENTS

WHEN I WAS first approached to write this book I thought, 'Yeah, nah.'

It was about two weeks after the announcement of my Fulbright scholarship, and the story had been picked up by news media in New Zealand and Australia. It was one of those feel-good, only-in-New Zealand stories — one of the *Tampa* kids had done something pretty decent.

Jenny Hellen, from Allen & Unwin, emailed me, and over lunch she laid out the idea of telling a story that was long overdue for telling. But the timing was less than ideal. I was about four weeks away from flying to the US to take up full-time postgraduate study. I was already to my neck in the unexpected and I knew I couldn't do justice to this extraordinary story if I didn't dedicate myself to it. I just couldn't do both.

Jenny was gracious in accepting my decision but noted that the offer remained open.

Fast forward to the start of 2020. I had adjusted to life in Washington and had my first semester of graduate school under my belt. With my partner Genevieve having relocated to Washington as well, we were in a good rhythm.

The thought of writing a book was still percolating in the back of my mind so I got in touch with Jenny around late February to resume discussions. Then, as we were going over the finer details of the writing process, the world went into Covid-19 lockdown. Suddenly, cooped up in our studio apartment, I had no excuses and all the time I needed to write the book.

I started old school, writing freehand in my journal before transferring my scribbles onto computer. Gradually, as the US descended into a semi-permanent lockdown, writing became an outlet for me. Through Zoom calls, WhatsApp messages and a timetable at the mercy of lockdown, we finally made it.

While I held the proverbial pen, this book would not have been possible without the support of my parents. I would call them in the late Washington evening, which was early morning in New Zealand, and we would talk for hours, with me asking a million questions to fill in the gaps in my knowledge. This book is dedicated to Mum and Dad, without whose strength, wisdom and courage I would not be where I am.

I want to thank my siblings — Hussein, Shekufah, Sakhi, Ali, Mojtaba and Mostafa — for their unwavering support throughout the process. We are a big family, full of drama, bickering and endless laughter. I wouldn't have it any other way. I hope this book makes you proud, and when people ask 'But where are you *really* from?' you can tell them to buy a copy.

I want to thank the *Tampa* refugees I consulted during writing, particularly Mehdi Azimi and Shah Wali Atayee. There are many others who remain anonymous but whose voices I hope I have carried throughout these pages. If it is not already clear, thank you to Captain Arne Rinnan, First Officer Christian Maltau and the crew of the MV *Tampa* who were courageous in their rescue, and compassionate in their hospitality. Thank you also to the team of volunteers who helped us navigate our first steps in Christchurch. Special thanks to Jan Clements for pulling together some of the finer details (and photos) of those early years at Ballantyne Avenue.

The *Tampa* is not my story. It is our story.

Writing this book required a long walk and a deep search down memory lane, which was not easy for me. I found it creatively and emotionally exhausting. But when I took up the challenge I knew I had to do the story justice. I hope I have done so.

Thank you to my friends in New Zealand, Australia, Washington and around the world who read individual chapters or offered advice in steering the entire process. Morwari Zafar, Niamatullah Ibrahimi, David Marr, Claire Higgins, Peter Lorimer, Garry Moore and Shuki — cheers to you all. Thank you to my friend Juan Zarama Perini for taking the cover photo.

This book would not have been possible without the team at Allen & Unwin, who believed in this story before I did. Jenny — thank you! Leonie Freeman, thank you for steering the ship. Rachel Scott, my editor, thank you for making sense of what I was trying to convey through my jumbled sentences.

Finally, I want to thank the woman who has stood beside me throughout the entire process. Thank you to Genevieve, my life partner, for your patience and not-so-gentle nudges to 'finish the book'. We would not be here without you.

And thank you to you, the reader, for choosing this book. I know the story is one that engenders passion and anger and other difficult emotions.

I welcome the conversations, grumblings and debates I hope the book manages to inspire.